In The Big Inning

THE FIRST BOOK BY JON BURNHAM

The Winning Pitch
First Printing 1995
Second Printing 1995

THE SECOND BOOK BY JON BURNHAM

In The Big Inning
First Printing 2008
Second Printing 2011
Third Printing 2014

In The Big Inning

Jon Burnham

HIS CALL
PRESS

Copyright © 2008 by Jon Burnham

In The Big Inning
by Jon Burnham

Printed in the United States of America

ISBN 978-1-60477-771-0

Dedication

I dedicate this book to my wife, Bev, our three children and their mates; Lee and Terry Burnham, Mark and Karen Burnham and Karl and Holly Figg.

Purpose

1. I wrote this book to honor God. I have watched the Lord change many lives through the scriptures, and I wanted to document the many different ways He made those changes.
2. Success is not what we've done, it's what we've done compared to what we could have done.

   I want the reader to put into practice these tried and tested Biblical standards, so they can experience the abundant life and success the Lord intended.

Contents

29 Innings

Foreword

This book is comprised of true stories and testimonies with names, ages, and locations modified so the reader will be free to learn from the Biblical standards that God used to change these lives. There are those individuals, recorded herein, who desired to have their identities known to acknowledge their appreciation for what the Lord did for them.

Acknowledgements

In deep appreciation, I acknowledge my Lord and Savior Jesus Christ for giving me direction to put into document form what He performed in the lives of the people recorded in this book.

I acknowledge how the Lord used my wife Bev, and her spiritual influence. Bev and I acknowledge and appreciate Sandy Kershaw for her valuable expertise editing this book.

We acknowledge how the Lord used our children; Lee, Mark and Holly, to help Bev and me grow in our faith. As they saw us at our worst, we watched the Lord develop each one to be the best child we could ever have.

Bev and I take great pleasure to acknowledge several key people who were used of God from the very beginning of our Christian lives. We thank the Lord for the late Dr Bruce Dunn, Dr. Walter Wilson, Dr. Bill Bright, Dr. Adrian Rogers, and Ruby Thompson.

We acknowledge Dr. Bill Gothard, Dr. Tim LaHaye, Dr. Steve Hauter, Dr. David Jeremiah, and Dave Wilkerson for their significant role helping Bev and me mature in the Lord. Bev was also influenced and personally helped by Verna Birkey.

Introduction

Having been a professional baseball pitcher I experienced many of the same things during a game that one experiences in the game of life itself. As you read, In The Big Inning, you will see many parallels as we use the analogy of baseball throughout this book. For instance, I use 'inning' instead of 'chapter' The game of life has time segments of minutes, hours, days, months while baseball has time segments separated by pitches, hits, walks, outs, innings.

In this game of life each one of us has experienced ups and downs, trials, mistakes, discouragements, good or bad consequences, blessings, exhilaration and everything else one can imagine. In the game of baseball a player can experience these same situations and emotions.

You don't have to be a baseball fan to appreciate the creativity of God as you recognize His Biblical principles in the following stories and illustrations.

You have heard that God loves baseball because He started the Bible, "In The Beginning". Since life itself and baseball are like a hand in glove, I titled this book, "In The Big Inning". Now that you have opened this book, your hand is in glove. These true stories will make the principles from God's Word provide a clear game plan to follow. God is the best coach we could ever have. I hope your game will improve as you read this playbook that will lead you to victory. So, 'let's play ball'.

Angry Player 'Subdued' First Inning

This first inning introduces you to a powerful story that documents what God did to help Mary, the wife of a very angry husband. God showed His power in one of the most unique ways that I have ever seen. You can learn from her experience and not let others control your emotions and mess up your game plan to glorify God.

Mary was going to divorce Jack, her angry husband. Jack would come home and verbally abuse her. His boss abused him all day, so when Jack came home he abuses Mary. She took the brunt of his wrath and finally had enough.

In order to help Mary look at this situation from God's point of view, I told her the following story, based on scripture, that was so profound I have used it many times with great results.

Bob went to see a counselor to get help concerning his anger. The counselor questioned him enough to be confident that Bob was a Christian. The counselor asked what made him so angry.

Bob said, "I started the day getting up late. Why? My wife, Janice forgot to set the alarm. So, I started the day being angry with her. Because I was late, I hurried while shaving and cut myself. I smelled burnt toast wafting up the stairs. I couldn't wait for another batch of toast, so I jumped in the car and backed out of the garage into the garbage cans. Janice put them out the night before so I didn't know they were there. I hit my head as I jumped out of the car and noticed, on my side of the car, the brand new tricycle I had just run over. By this time I'm in a rage. I heaved the bike over the car into the front yard and almost hit the family cat. The kids ran into the house yelling, 'Mom! Mom! Dad's trying to kill our cat. My wife raced out of the house yelling at me. There was garbage all over the place and everyone was screaming. I jumped back in the car, and tore off up the street. I was finally headed for work. Two blocks away from home a little old lady backed out of her drive way in front of me hogging the middle of the road, and proceeded to putt along about 20 miles an hour. I could not get around her. I finally arrived at work, and my secretary said, 'where have you been all day?' Now I was mad at my secretary for sounding like a snip. She informed me that Janice had called. I asked, 'what does she want?' The secretary said, 'you left your briefcase at home.' What do you see in all this?"

The counselor said, "I see two things. One, you are a liar, and two; you are the ugliest man I have ever seen." Bob jumped out of his chair, reached across the desk to grab the counselor and said, "You're just another one who ticks me off."

The counselor reached into his desk drawer and took out a pistol. He pointed the gun at Bob and told him to sit down. Bob immediately did so.

Bob asked, in a rather subdued voice, 'what kind of counselor are you?'

The counselor said, "I just wanted to see if you could control yourself, in the midst of your rage, when faced with a greater power. You did stop. Bob, you're not the ugliest man

I've ever seen. I just wanted to see if I could get you upset with me."

The counselor continued, "Bob, you told me you're a Christian. If you are a Christian why aren't you yielding to God's greater power inside you? Are you a liar? As a Christian you have within you the dynamite power of resurrection. That's more powerful than this gun, that's empty, by the way. You have been letting everyday circumstances rule your life. It says in 1John 4:4 ..... He who is in you is greater than he who is in the world. (NKJV) You have been living beneath your God given privileges."

Bob was convicted and rededicated his life to the Lord in prayer right then and there. The Lord grants all Christians the power to show this skeptical world how great He is. If we don't draw upon the power of God, at those opportune times, we miss the blessing of experiencing His power. Your response is very obvious to those watching. Your proper response can draw others to Him. This is where your life can reach another life. What an honor to properly represent Him, and then give Him the credit for what He did.

After telling Mary this story I asked her to do something I have never asked anyone to do before or since. I told her to go to the variety store, buy a squirt gun and put it in her purse. I said, "When Jack comes home, and starts yelling at you, give him the squirt gun and tell him to shoot you. As your hair gets wet and your makeup runs down your face, he'll probably ask, 'why are you having me do this?' Be ready to show him your real power, which I explained to her how to use.

A few weeks later Mary came back and said, "Jack came home and started his rant, so I reached in my purse, handed him my squirt gun and told him to shoot me. Jack started squirting me.

Then he asked, 'Why are you having me do this?'

I told him, "I've been wrong for allowing your puny squirt gun power to drive me to an attorney to get a divorce. Will you forgive me for not yielding to the dynamite, resurrection power of God in my life?" I can do all things through Christ who strengthens me. I purpose to stay with you, and show you the power of God in my life. Maybe someday you too will experience God's power, and what it's all about."

She said, "Jack broke down and cried. He saw the love and power of God in my life.

He asked, 'How can I have what you have?'

I explained the gospel the best way I knew how, and Jack asked Jesus to come into his life.

Jon, I'm so happy. Jack can really love me now. This will be the first time, since we've been married."

Perhaps one day Jack's boss will see the power within Jack and trust Christ himself. Jack knows that, in comparison to Jesus, his employer has only squirt gun power'.

Which of the two powers control your life? Is it God's power or the puny power of someone else? I've come to realize that when I let another person control my emotions, I've let that person be my God. The first commandment tells us that we should have no other gods before us. If you want to show someone that you are using the power of God in your life, hand that person a squirt gun.

2ⁿᵈ Inning

Suicide Bunt Came 'Alive'

What happens when a person makes a threat to keep you in line? Mass murder and suicide could have been the result of a threat made by Al to his wife Carrie just after they were married. Any one of us can say the wrong thing, and others can get caught up focusing on what we said and make wrong choices. During this inning Carrie and Al were headed for death, yet the Lord kept these players alive. See what the Lord did to get their focus on Him and change their minds.

Carrie came to me at break time during the seminar I was giving. She told me she was filled with guilt for what she had been doing for the last six months with a neighbor.

I said, "Please explain."

Carrie stated that when they were married Al told her that if she ever had an affair he would kill her, the guy, their families, and then turn the gun on himself.

Carrie is a Christian, but she had fallen into deep sin. As she listened to me speak, she became more and more convicted about her affair. She told me that Al's job took him out of the area all week, and he was only home on weekends.

Carrie and Al lived in the country. Their neighbors lived just a mile away. The neighbor's wife worked during the day and her husband worked second shift.

Carrie explained, "Here we were. I was home alone all week, and so was the neighbor. This thing developed into more than a friendship. Tonight you gave an example about someone putting a sign up in front of their big window that read, 'don't throw rocks.' You said, 'I'd begin to look for rocks. I know it's wrong, but when someone tells me not to do something, I tend to consider it.' Jon, when you said that, I remembered what Al told me not to do. I know I should never have become involved with our neighbor, but I have to admit Al's comment triggered my lower nature. Now I'm in real trouble. My focus was definitely wrong. I'm not blaming Al. I realize what I've done and it all came crashing down on me tonight.

She said, "Here is my real problem," as she began to cry, "Now that I've been involved with that neighbor, I don't know what to do. I have felt guilty for a long time. I can't stand myself! I have no other alternative, but go home tonight and kill myself. If I tell Al what I've done, I know what he'll do. He's already told me. This is why I had to tell you what I'm going to do tonight. There is no other way. I can't go on like this anymore!"

I knew that scripture tells us that God will give us within that hour what to say. She was looking at her situation with the human logic thinking through to the wrong conclusion.

I had to say something, so I asked the Lord in prayer, "What would you have me say to this woman?" He gave me a view that made sense to me.

I told Carrie, "Scripture says that Satan wants us to keep on sinning, or he wants us dead. Satan knows scripture. He quoted it to Jesus in the book of Matthew chapter four. Satan sees that it says in Revelation 1:18b … And I have the keys of Hades and of Death. (NKJV)

"Since the Lord holds the keys of death, Satan would love to see you try to take your key out of God's hand, and tell Him when you're going to die. If he can influence you to do that, you would be playing God. Satan tried to be like God when he was the highest created angel named Lucifer. He said in Isaiah 14:14 'I will ascend above the heights of the clouds; I will be like the most High.' (NKJV) Satan was thrown out of heaven for playing that game. He suffered a huge consequence; therefore, he figures you will too. That's his goal because he hates you. Why? Because you were born in God's image."

"Let's think for a minute. Satan wants you to sin or die, and yet the Lord wants you to obey Jesus and live. That's quite a difference. Which sounds the best to you? Since the Lord is convicting you to do the right thing and confess, I'm sure He will give Al the grace he needs to receive your repentance! I believe God is doing all this to set you free. Confessing to God and to Al is scriptural. It says in Acts 24:16 'This being so, I myself always strive to have a conscience without offense toward God and men.' (NKJ)"

"Both you and I know that I'm not the Holy Spirit, therefore, please don't think for a minute that I know God's timing on this. It is never too late to obey the One who loved you enough to die for you; to wash your sins away. I'll call my wife tonight, and we will pray for you and Al."

I called Bev and shared with her every detail about Carrie's, distress. I told Bev I'd get back to her as soon as I knew anything else.

After talking with the Lord and Bev, I went right to sleep. The next morning I turned on the news and noticed that there was no report of suicide or a mass murder. I didn't know anymore until that night. I continued on with the seminar, and at break time Al and Carrie came up to me. She was hanging on his arm, looking up at him admiringly. Al smiled and said, "Thank you, Jon, for encouraging my wife to trust

God and tell me what she's been doing. When she told me, I said that I knew something wasn't right. I didn't want to believe what my spirit was telling me. I immediately asked her forgiveness for putting up "the sign", as you put it, 'Don't you dare have an affair.' I know she was wrong in what she did, but I was wrong in putting up that sign. I was gone too much and didn't protect her as I should have."

What a wonderful blessing it was to see Al's supernatural response and to see Carrie obey as she did to clear her conscience with God and her husband. Now she is truly alive! I'm so thankful to the Lord for helping me speak up in His behalf and not try to side step the issue. The Lord gave me the courage to trust Him to deal with this potentially explosive situation. God displayed His power to us all.

Back home several months later, the doorbell rang. I opened it, and there they were; Al, Carrie and their three children. Al told me that he and Carrie wanted to give me permission to use their names, and to tell their story, if I thought it would help others. They were on their way to live in another part of the country and start over.

We thank you, Al and Carrie. I have used your name and your story several times, and it has brought Godly results. God has blessed you both.

Have you been threatened? The principle in this story is focus on the Lord and not the threat. Follow Jesus and not your lower nature to do what it begs you to do.

If you focus on the threat, the results could match what happened to Carrie. She saw death as the answer. I hope you are encouraged to be prayed up and to trust the Holy Spirit when you find yourself looking at a potential death situation. You never know in what inning of life you will be called up to the plate to face the enemy. It says in Eph 6:12 'For we are not fighting against people made of flesh and blood, but against persons without bodies—the evil rulers of the unseen world, those mighty satanic beings and great evil princes of darkness who rule this world; and against huge numbers of wicked spirits in the spirit world.' That evil power is as real today as when it was recorded in the Bible years ago. God's power is available to us as well and remember, Jesus defeated sin, death and the devil when He gave His life for you and me on the cross.

3ʳᵈ Inning

'<u>Conference</u>' In the Dugout

I'll never forget the time God called me into the dugout to teach me a lesson. I had been using man's way to correct man's problem of communication. God used only a part of one verse to correct poor communication. As you read this you may see some things you have tried, only to find that they didn't work until you did what the Lord told you to do. Chuck was ready to take his own life because the communication with his wife was so bad, but God told Chuck what to do and he did it.

Over the years I've been asked to speak on the subject of communication. At this conference I gave one hundred suggestions to help those in attendance successfully communicate. As the conference came to a close I realized time had run out, and I had only shared half of my suggestions; but many attendees told me they had heard enough to successfully communicate with their mates.

Three months later I received a call from Chuck, one of the men who had attended that conference. He asked if I would come back and speak on communication again. Chuck said he soon discovered that he and some others were falling back into the same habits of communication. They wanted the rest of those communication gems I had not given. We set the date, and I looked forward to it.

Once there, I renewed friendships with these wonderful people. I shared the other fifty ways to communicate. We had another great evening, and everyone agreed again that having all one hundred ways to properly communicate would truly work.

Sometime later, I received another call from Chuck. He said, "Communication with my wife is in the pits!" He asked if they could please have another communication conference. Chuck felt like killing himself if the communication with his wife got any worse. He told me just how he intended to end his life. I met Chuck for lunch, and we set a date for still another conference. Obviously, I was discouraged. Bev and I prayed about what to bring to the next conference. After all a man's life was at stake.

After praying with Bev, I received some new and different thoughts. I don't hear voices, but the thoughts can be understood as though the Lord was speaking to my mind from the equity of His scripture. That must be what the scripture means as it relates to, "a still small voice." The ideas come in such a way that it seems as though you have had a conversation with the Lord.

I said, "Lord, I don't know what happened. Why did the first two conferences fail? Many people told me they were confident that they would do better.

The Lord said, "Jon, when you see that a person is ready to become a Christian, what then? Do you lift up one hundred ways to get to me or do you lift me up?"

I said, "I lift you up."

He said, "Then what do I do?"

I said, "You draw them to yourself like you said in John 12:32 …' if I be lifted up from the earth, will draw all *men* unto me.'" (NKJV)

"Jon, when the call came for you to give the first two conferences on communication what did you lift up?"

I said, "I lifted up communication skills."

Then He said, "This third conference I want you to lift me up in my rightful place, and I will help the people communicate."

I said, "How do I lift you up like that?"

He said, "Simply use my Word. I'm going to give you just a part of one verse that will be enough to help the people communicate."

I asked, "What is the verse, Lord?"

His spirit inspired me to dig into His word, and I felt confident that He would show me the verse.

The main thing I learned from this personal thought time with Jesus was that I had left Him out altogether and used man's ideas on how to communicate better. God is the One that should be lifted up to draw people back to Him.

As I continued reading the Bible, I came across a verse that jumped right off the page. Matthew 25:40 '........., inasmuch as you did it to one of the least of these My brethren, you did it to Me.' (NKJV)

The Lord was gracious to me, and to those in the conference, as He patiently waited to be lifted up. Even though I went to the third conference with just part of a verse, I had tremendous confidence that I was going to see the Lord do what man could not do. I didn't know how this was going to play out since the people, most likely, expected a ton more information to correct their problems with communication.

Previously I had used one hundred of man's ideas. God used a part of a verse. God desire for us to call upon Him in every situation so He can show us His power to correct a problem or to win a battle. After all, who can run your life better than the One who created you? God only used three hundred soldiers instead of thousands to win the battle for Gideon in Judges 7:20,Then the three companies blew the trumpets and broke the pitchers—they held the torches in their left hands and the trumpets in their right hands for blowing—and they cried, "The sword of the LORD and of Gideon!"

In this next inning I explain what happened to Chuck.

4ᵗʰ Inning

Chuck Slid Into '<u>Third</u>' and Came '<u>Home</u>' to Score

The principle you will observe in this inning is that God gives His power to the humble. Sometimes He has to humble us in order to give us His power to understand that His ways are best. We'll leave those two failed retreats behind and let's see how Chuck came home from third base, (from this third retreat), to score. I used part of a verse that God gave me for this conference. If you do what the people did in this inning, your communication will also improve.

Meeting the people for the third time on the same subject was humbling. The Lord was working on me; therefore, I knew He would get through to the attendees.

I was pumped because I knew that His ways are worth finding out. I had great confidence in His confidence in Himself to help us all communicate better.

After opening in prayer, I told those in attendance what I had learned, "God honors His word, therefore; that's what we are going to use. We are going to use just part of a verse. This part will improve your communication with your mate and with other people as well."

I shared with them that it was my fault for lifting up one hundred ways to communicate instead of lifting up the Lord by showing, from scripture, what He could do through His word.

I opened the Bible and turned to Matthew 25:40 'Assuredly, I say to you, inasmuch as you did it to one of the least of these My brethren, you did it to Me.' NKJV "This will take care of your communication problems", I stated.

Chuck spoke up, "Jon, I had such hopes that this conference would give me the answer I needed. I guess it's not going to happen. How in the world could that verse help me improve communication with anyone, let alone my wife? Isn't that scripture telling me that I'm supposed to treat my wife, as though she's Jesus? Most of the time, my wife doesn't act like Jesus, so how can I honestly treat her as though she is? Wouldn't I have to lie to myself to do that? Does God want me to lie?"

This is where he slid into third base (third retreat) screaming all the way. Chuck's wife was embarrassed, and everyone there was feeling for her. I hadn't planned on him, or anyone in this retreat, throwing me for a loop like this. After all, I believed the Lord had given this scripture to use for this meeting. Another scripture came to mind found in Matt 10:19 'For it will be given to you in that hour what you should speak;' (NKJV) I threw up a silent prayer to God on the spot. "Lord! I didn't count on this. I need your help here. He made a very logical point. I feel embarrassed for his wife."

I received a thought, and I didn't have time to mull it over. I just blurted out, "Flip the verse over."

Chuck asked, "How do you flip a verse over?"

I didn't know, so I threw up another silent prayer to God and asked, "How do I flip the verse over?" A thought came, and I said. "Chuck, how am I to view you? The Lord says to me in that verse, "Jon, inasmuch as you did it to one of the least of these My brethren, you did it to Me.' Therefore Chuck, how am I to view you?"

Chuck said, "You are to view me, as though I'm Christ."

I said, "That's right. This is how you are to flip the verse over. When your wife is acting badly, be like Christ to her. When she is acting like Christ, treat her as though she is Christ. I'm viewing you as though you are Christ. I would expect you to be Christ like to your wife when she is not acting like Christ to you. None of us can get away from that verse. This scripture translates to the wives in the same way."

Then the Lord gave me more insight from scripture. I told the audience that the reasonable question to ask is, "Why can't we communicate successfully with one another? Could it be that we have violated our marriage vows?" You might defend yourself and say, 'How can that be? I have been faithful to my mate.' I said to the group, "We can violate our marriage vows in a number of ways."

I continued, "I violated my marriage vow to God just a few minutes after Bev and I left the wedding reception. We jumped in the car headed for the first stop of our honeymoon when I realized that I left my watch at my parent's house."

Going back home was the opposite direction of going on our honeymoon, so I made an anger inspired 'U' turn and headed home, speeding all the way. I put on my watch and raced back to the car and noticed Bev was crying. I said, "Hey, what's the matter with you? This is a happy day!'

She said, "I married the wrong one."

I had just violated my marriage vow to God and to Bev. I vowed that, 'I would love, honor, and cherish her!' Were my actions loving, honoring and cherishing? No! Absolutely not!

The people at this retreat understood. I'm sure each couple had violated their marriage vow to God, one way or another, during their marriage. What happens when we violate our marriage vow? The Bible tells us in Ecclesiastes 5:4-7 'So when you talk to God and vow to Him that you will do something, don't delay in doing it, for God has no pleasure in fools. Keep your promise to him.

It is far better not to say you'll do something than to say you will and then not do it. In that case, your mouth is making you sin. Don't try to defend yourself by telling the messenger from God that it was all a mistake to make the vow. That would make God very angry; and he might destroy your prosperity.' (TLB)

When we violate a marriage vow God uses the least amount of discipline possible to bring us in line. The most loving thing He does is not to allow us to communicate successfully. Why would He do that? I believe He wants us to see that there are consequences when we don't keep our vow to Him. He also wants to get our attention as to why we violated our marriage vow.

Could the answer be that we left our first love for Jesus? If that's it, we don't have His power to keep our vow to Him, to love our mate, or to be able to communicate.

When we put anything or anyone above Jesus, we have replaced Him. Replacing Him is like putting Him on the shelf. God is a jealous God. He said He would share His glory with no man. He is jealous for our good. If He had helped the people communicate better after the first two retreats, they would have put Him further back on the shelf by not needing Him. After all, they had all these man made ways to communicate, but God could not let man's ways work.

Discipline is the same root word for disciple. When that Christian person is disciplined by God to say, no to what's wrong and yes to what's right, that person is a disciple of Christ.

The Lord begins His instruction to husbands and wives in Ephesians 5:18 'And do not be drunk with wine, in which is dissipation; but be filled with the Spirit.' (NKJV)

He has commanded, in Eph 5:18, to put Him first. He is a jealous God for our good. He knows we will not have much to offer others unless He is first place in our lives.

This retreat ended with a spirit of confidence in the Lord. The proof is in the scripture. A few months after the third conference we found out why we didn't need a fourth.

Chuck came to see me. He said, "I wanted to tell you that you won't have to worry about me taking my own life."

I said, "Great! Tell me about it."

He said, "I was watching my wife do something that really ticks me off. She's a bird watcher and was oblivious to my special plants and flowers, and she was walking all over the ones I had just planted. I raced to the back door to yell at her. She would have come in and we would have argued, but I heard that still small voice you talk about.

The voice said, 'Wait a minute. If that were Jesus walking in the garden, would you yell at Him?'

I knew I wouldn't do that. I had immediate peace. Then my human mind kicked in. Jesus would know better. I gulped for air to yell at my wife when that same voice said, 'Wait a minute. Isn't this a opportunity to be Christ like to her? Would Jesus yell at her?"

He said he walked out to his wife, picked her up, hugged and kissed her. He had little regard for the plants now because he was under the Lord's control. He said he was thrilled to actually experience what happens when you are faithful to flip the verse over. He explained to his wife how he slid into the third conference fighting the scriptural concept. With this experience in his own back yard, he was ecstatic with the joy of victory. In other words, he jumped up after sliding into third, and he came on home to score for the Lord.

Can you see how your communication will improve by living Matt 25:40? Please don't use man's way to do what only God can do. Humble yourself and God will give you power. Let people see Jesus in your life. That's the way we lift Him up. He will draw others to you and to Himself. Keep Jesus first in your life by viewing other people as though they are Christ. Remember: His power enables us to be like Christ to others. Jesus Christ can help each one of us score for Him in this game.

5th Inning

In The Lineup

Have you ever driven into the car wash and found the line was a mile long? To make things worse, you can't back out to go your merry way. This happened to me. Being stuck in line like that was frustrating for me, but it became a blessing in disguise. That irritating experience was used by God to illuminate His word to me. You either let irritations eat you alive, or you watch God's creativity go into action to teach you something.

Since I was stuck, I pulled out my Living New Testament and started to read Mark 4:24-25 'And be sure to put into practice what you hear. The more you do this, the more you will understand what I tell you. To him who has shall be given; from him who has not shall be taken away even what he has.'

I thought, "Wait a minute. This sounds like a riddle. What is the meaning of this verse?" I didn't have a seminary background, so I asked the Holy Spirit, the one who wrote it. After all, the Lord said He wrote this through holy men as the Holy Spirit inspired them. In John 14:26 'But when the Father sends the Comforter instead of me and by the Comforter I mean the Holy Spirit—he will teach you much, as well as remind you of everything I myself have told you.' (TLB)

As I was reading this over and over, I realized the tension was gone that had built up in me just a moment before when I saw I was trapped in this long line of cars. Now I was caught up in the reading of His word, and I hoped the line wouldn't go so fast that I wouldn't have time to figure out what this verse meant. God can turn things around so fast when we focus on Him.

Mark 4: 24 "Be sure to put into practice what you hear. The more you do this the more you will understand what I tell you." OK! If you put into practice what you hear, you get rewarded with understanding.

Then He says in verse 25 "From those who have not, from him shall be taken away even what he has." Oh! What you have is what you heard. In other words, you will have taken away what you heard if you don't put it into practice. Also you will forget what you heard if you don't put that into practice. Wow. God, you are so good.

I was really excited about the Holy Spirit getting something through to me directly from His word. Therefore, we start every Family Focus Seminar with Mark 4:24-25. I saw the significance of encouraging the people to come, and hear what the Lord is saying; then put that into practice. They will forget what they heard if they don't; thus, miss out on more understanding.

I became very thankful that the car wash line was so long. I had a chance to put into practice what I had read in the Bible, and that was to learn patience. It says in James 1:2-4 'Dear brothers, is your life full of difficulties and temptations? Then be happy, for when the way is rough, your patience has a chance to grow. So let it grow, and don't try to squirm out of your problems. For when your patience is finally in full bloom, then you will be ready for anything, strong in character, full and complete.' (TLB)

Just think, moments ago I wanted to squirm out of the problem of being caught in the car wash line. Pretty short inning, huh? Well, once you are in the line up, it doesn't take long to notice that this game flies by, especially when you're having fun. I don't care what inning we're in; this game of life is very interesting.

You ask Jesus a question, and He's right there to give you His answer. He's the One to listen to. Jesus is the only one who can help you win the game. If you know Him as your Savior and Lord you know what I mean. If you don't know Jesus as your Savior and Lord, please read on. I pray He draws you to Himself as He is lifted up in this book. You will read more and more about how He changed my life and the lives about whom I'm writing.

6th Inning

Three Drunks Called Out

Afters I became a Christian, I was excited to be able to pitch for Jesus instead of pitching for me as I had been doing as a non-Christian. Have you had times when you spoke up for Jesus only to find out later that you may have wasted your time? Hopefully, this chapter will encourage you and perhaps inspire you even more, to share Christ with others.

One evening I spoke to a group of teens, and five guys asked Christ into their lives. The following weekend three of the five were drunk out of their minds. I was discouraged especially since I was a novice, so I went to see Don Ingram, a minister who lived just a few miles away.

Don said, "The reason you are discouraged is because you believe you didn't get three of the five saved good enough. I know just how you feel. I had twins come forward in a meeting I was holding, and one of them went to the mission field; the other went to jail. If I want to feel good about myself, I think about the twin who is on the mission field. If I want to humble myself, as the Lord calls us to do, I simply remember the twin that's in jail.

Don told me to look at life from God's point of view. I'm going to share what Don told me in the form of pitches that any of us can throw. I will call them the "three winning pitches." These three pitches helped keep me enthusiastically sharing my faith in Jesus all these years.

The 1st 'Winning Pitch is what I call, 'Choose'.

God threw that choice pitch when He chose to love us. He didn't have to love us, since we are recognized as sinners. He tells us in Rom 3:23 "for all have sinned and fall short of the glory of God." (NKJ)

Jesus threw that pitch many times.

1. Jesus chose to leave His heavenly estate and come to earth to give His life for us so we could have eternal life.

2. Jesus chose to obey in the temple when his parents asked Him why he didn't join them on the caravan back home. Jesus asked, "Didn't you know that I must be about my father's business?" It's interesting that part of His Father's business was to obey His earthly parents, so He went with them and was subject to them.

3. Jesus threw the choose pitch when He chose to yield to His Father three times in the Garden of Gethsemane. Three times He said, "Not my will, but thy will be done."

4. Right after that He yielded and chose to go to the cross in obedience to His Father.

5. He wasn't done throwing that winning pitch because He chose to stay on the cross unto death. He chose not to call the legions of angels down to take Him off the cross even though He had done nothing wrong.

We can thank Him every day for throwing that wonderful pitch time after time. The importance of that pitch is brought out in I Sam 15:22, "to obey is better than sacrifice," (NKJV)

If Jesus had not chosen to obey, there would be no sacrifice. If there had been no sacrifice there would not be salvation. By following Jesus, we have made the right choice! He will help us make right choices.

Don asked me, "Why did you ask Jesus to be your Savior?"

I said, "Some dear friends of ours, Maurice and Opal Stahly invited us to hear General Harrison speak. The General was one of the men who signed the Second World War Peace Treaty. Quoting the Bible, He said that 'all have sinned and fall short of the glory of God.' The General stated, 'This means your Dad, Mom, brother, sister, aunt, uncle, Sunday School teacher, minister and the librarian etc. I thought, 'Librarian?' He covered about everyone. I had to admit; it includes me. In addition, General Harrison mentioned what it says in Rev 3:20 'Behold, I stand at the door and knock. If anyone hears My voice and opens the door, I will come in to him.' (NKJV)

"I did choose to obey His call; therefore, I opened the door of my heart and received Jesus Christ as my Savior and Lord."

Don asked, "What if you had not chosen to open the door?"

I replied, "I would not have become a Christian at that point. I just wanted what God was offering me. I loved me too much to want to go to hell. I loved me so much I wanted to go to heaven. I found out later that God created me with the love that I have for myself. I appreciate what Jesus did for me when I was still this cocky, egotistical, foul-mouthed punk. The Bible tells me that while I was yet a sinner He loved me enough to die for me and take my place on the cross. Love sure does beget love. I just wanted to love Him back, so I opened the door of my heart to receive Him."

Don asked, "What about those five guys? Each one of them chose to obey by opening the door."

"Why did you grow?"

I said, "Because I chose to follow Jesus."

He stated, "Now about the three you are questioning. God chastens every one of His own. He doesn't spank neighbor children, He only spanks His own. He knows by looking in their hearts if they were serious about wanting Him to be their Savior and Lord. He's the only one who knows. We read in I John 2:3-6 'And how can we be sure that we belong to him? By looking within ourselves: are we really trying to do what he wants us to? Someone may say, 'I am a Christian; I am on my way to heaven; I belong to Christ.' But if he doesn't do what Christ tells him to, he is a liar. But those who do what Christ tells them to learn to love God more and more. That is the way to know whether or not you are a Christian. Anyone who says he is a Christian should live as Christ did. (TLB)

Don said, "If those three are really His, He will chasten them. God will use His Word, H.S., you, and others in the lives of those five boys. The Word points out in Rom 8:5 "Those who (Choose) to let themselves be controlled by their lower natures live only to please themselves, but those who (Choose) to follow after the Holy Spirit find themselves doing those things that please God."

Choose is the 1st Winning Pitch. We know that everyone makes choices; therefore, everyone throws that pitch. Have you chosen to trust Jesus, and do you choose to obey Him?

Next, Don gave me a principle that I like to call Love, the 2nd winning pitch.

Jesus threw that pitch first - He loved me first. We find in 1J4: 19 We love Him because He first Loved us. (NKJV)

He showed me how to throw the pitch of love.

Don said, "I will never burn out!"

I asked, 'Why?"

Don asked, "Do you have a game plan?"

I said, "To Witness and Disciple."

Don asked, "Why do you Witness?"

I said, "To see people come to Christ."

He said, "Those are results. I used to do that, but I don't do that anymore."

I stated, "You witness, so what do you mean?"

He answered, "Yes, I still witness, but not for the results."

He asked, "Jon, Why do you disciple people?"

I said, "So they can grow and lead others to Christ."

Don said, "Those are results; I used to do that, but I don't do that anymore either."

Then he gave a profound answer. He said, "I witness now, and I disciple now, because I love Jesus. Therefore, I will never burn out! Jon, if you witness and disciple people because you love Jesus, you will never burn out." Leave the results with God.

I gave the first two pitches a name, but you will see that the third pitch is unique.

The Word is the 3rd winning pitch. - It says in Ps 138:2 "For You have magnified Your Word above all Your name." (NKJV)

The Word 'Is' the Pitch.

J 1:1-4 & 14 -"In the beginning was the Word, and the Word was with God, and the Word was God. He was in the beginning with God. All things were made through Him, and without Him nothing was made that was made. In Him was life, and the life was the light of men. And the Word became flesh and dwelt among us. NKJV)

Jesus is the power pitch. It says in Heb 4:12 For the word of God is living and powerful, and sharper than any two-edged sword, piercing even to the division of soul and spirit, and of joints and marrow, and is a discerner of the thoughts and intents of the heart. (NKJV) Jesus wants us to throw this pitch over home plate so the one to whom we are pitching will see Jesus in our lives. A life reaches a life.

When you read, memorize, and meditate on the Word of God, you are making the greatest investment that can be made in the One who wrote the Word. That investment builds a treasure in the Lord. Your heart will go where your treasure is; meaning, your heart will go and stay with Jesus as you read and invest in His Word. You will keep your first love instead of losing your first love as mentioned in Revelation. 2:4 "Nevertheless I have *this* against you, that you have left your first love." NKJV (When a husband invests in his wife, his treasure builds up there and his heart stays with her.)

We've all heard the comment, "If that guy's a Christian, I don't want any part of Christianity!" Paul had a unique slant on this in II Thes 3:9 (Jon Paraphrased) That Christian guy has his eyes on the world. You become like what you focus on. If you keep focusing on him, you will become like him! Paul said, "Don't look at him; look at us. Our eyes are on Jesus. See the difference? We're following Jesus. Do what we're doing. Focus on Jesus and you will become like Jesus."

Don not only helped me learn about these three pitches for myself, I was better equipped to help those three guys that were drunk. Ministering to teens helped me grow in the Lord. As God taught me, I passed on to them what I learned from the Bible. If they live their lives because they love Jesus, they won't burn out either.

Don has had a profound influence on me. His life influenced me! A life reaches a life! I saw those three winning pitches in his advice to me.

After I met Don, another set of twins came to one of his meetings. One of those twin brothers trusted Jesus as his Savior and Lord that night. A few nights later those same twins came to a meeting I was conducting. The other twin brother came forward and gave his life to Christ. Both those boys, grown men now, went to the mission field for a season of time.

Each one who reads this story has a sphere of influence and is influencing others right now. Many people are watching you. Are you throwing those three pitches, choose, love, and the Word?

Your influence is powerful and far reaching. There are those who know you have this book. They know that you have the Bible. Are you living in such a way that others will want what you have? Lift up Jesus in your life by reading the Bible and by all means, live it out.

Can you think back and pinpoint the ones God used to influence you to become a Christian. Will others point to you and say that you were the one who was used of God to direct them to the truth?

You will make choices the rest of your life. You can choose to love the Word", that is, if you haven't made that choice already. I'm willing to guess that you have. When you're done with this book, give it to someone else and use the power of influence God has already given you.

7ᵗʰ Inning

What's Your 'Level' Of Play?

Do you want to make top-level decisions? Do you know on what level you are playing this game? This inning will help you see right where you are when you make decisions. If you make decisions on the level that God wants, you will be very successful. Jimmy was making decisions that were failing and it almost cost him his marriage. You will see Jimmy's level of play that will encourage you not to go there. Jimmy found the level that turned his life around.

Jimmy's wife requested that he call me to see if he could improve his game. She was in hopes that during the game he was playing, he would make right decisions at home and in the workplace.

Jimmy, who was in his early fifties, was having an affair with a woman in her twenties. She wanted the security she assumed he could give her, and Jimmy believed that he was still young and handsome enough to be captivating to most any woman. All his children were grown and on their own. He was about to leave his wife, but he chose to honor his wife's request and come in to see me.

Jimmy came into my counseling office showing confidence that this session was not going to go anywhere. He had a winning way, and my heart went out to him. He could tell I was genuinely interested in him and his situation.

Jimmy wanted to get this session over with, so he could tell his wife that he had gone to counselling, and it didn't work. He told me about the other woman and how natural their relationship seemed. They just hit it off, and she was so easy to talk with. He had had no intention of becoming involved, but he experienced a youthful rush each time he saw her. Jimmy would say to himself, "See, I'm not too old to attract a younger woman." The younger woman must have thought, "What a handsome, mature man. He has done well in life. I admire that. He could provide me with security, and he thinks I'm attractive.

He said the relationship had gotten out of hand, and now he was emotionally involved. He knew he was wrong because, as a Christian, he was fighting the conviction of God. Jimmy thought that he could witness to this young woman. He figured she was not a Christian because of the way she talked and acted. He knew that he was not being a good testimony by coming on to her, but he logically thought through to the wrong conclusion. You see, Jimmy was on the immature level of decision-making, which was sure to fail.

As we talked, he told me that every decision that anyone makes is based on fear of loss and desire for gain. Jimmy said, "I wanted to gain this other woman. I didn't fear losing my wife. As a result, I'm going for the gain. You see, Jon, everyone makes decisions on that same basis. Think it through; what decisions have you made that don't line up with what I'm saying?"

I said, "When you invest in someone or something your treasure builds up there, and where your treasure is, there will your heart be also." He said, "That sounds like scripture. I've heard that before." I said, "Yes, you got that right. It's in Luke 12:34 For where your treasure is, there will your heart be also. (NKJV)"

Jimmy, you said, 'Every decision we make is based on fear of loss and desire for gain."

"On what level did you make the decision to keep going with that woman?" You are right about every decision we make is based on fear of loss and desire for gain, but did you know that there are three levels in that decision making process?

He asked, "What levels are you talking about?"

I said, "The first level is, I fear my loss, and I desire my gain, which is known as the immature level of decision-making. It's the all about me level. The second level is a maturing level. I fear the loss of someone else. I desire the gain of someone else."

Jimmy said, "Then I'm making my decisions based on fearing my girlfriend's loss and desiring her gain. It shows I'm thinking of someone else, am I not?"

I said, "Yes, you are, and that shows you are not on the immature level of decision making, but you will not be successful on this second level. The girlfriend will look to you for what she wants and needs. You will be her god. She will be looking to you for her sustenance. You said you wanted to witness to her. Ask yourself, 'what kind of a god am I? Am I a good god, or am I a bad god for her?'

Now you have to come through for her. How do you feel about playing the role of god in her life?"

He looked upset, but said nothing; therefore, I went on to add to his basic premise of decision-making. I said, "When you make a choice on God's level, the highest level, that decision will be based on fearing God's loss and desiring His gain. On this level the decisions you make could glorify the Lord. The bonus is that God will take care of all three levels. He will be glorified on His level; He will take care of your wife and others on the second level; in addition, He will take care of you on your personal level. I encourage you to make decisions on the top level."

When Jimmy left my office, I wondered if he would ever be back. He did come back a week later, and his hand was all bandaged up.

I ask what had happened to his hand.

He said, "I was so mad at you, I went out to the car and slammed my fist against the steering wheel. I felt like I broke it. It still hurts."

I asked him why he was so angry.

Jimmy replied, "Because you were right! A third level decision brought me back in here. I do want to glorify God."

I took him back to the premise that when you invest in someone your heart will go there. I asked Jimmy, "Do you remember when you stopped investing in your wife and began investing in the other woman? Since this is a principle from God's word, I'm sure your heart will go back to your wife as you begin to invest in her again. The best way to start investing in your wife is to clear your conscience with God, your wife and that other woman. You made a vow to God that you would forsake all others. Your wife heard the vow you made to God when you were married. The vow was made to God, and He is holding you to it. With a clear conscience, He will give you the power to keep the vow. Your wife was to benefit from your vow to God. You need to ask your wife to forgive you. Then, if it's all right with your wife, have her by your side when you phone the other woman. Tell the woman that you have rededicated yourself to Jesus and to your marriage, and you were wrong to have developed a relationship with her. Ask the woman to forgive you."

Jimmy said, "Why should I ask her to forgive me since it was my wife that I offended?"

I said, "You harmed the other woman too."

"How?" he asked.

I said, "You gave her the wrong picture of what Christianity is all about. You have the responsibility to ask her to forgive you for that. You were after what wasn't yours. Asking her to forgive you will be the first thing you will have done, in your relationship with her, to glorify the Lord. To ask her to forgive you is a top-level decision. God will be honored by your decision and will bless the woman, your wife and you. He blesses all three levels when you make a decision on His level. The Bible says in I Cor. 10:31 ... "

"What ever you do, do all to the glory of God." TLB What you were doing was not glorifying God.

Jimmy was obedient to God and did all the above on God's level. I admire him for that. Jimmy reunited with his wife and God blessed him for having been obedient. I thank God for showing us the need to make decisions on His level, fearing God's loss and desiring God's gain.

What's your level of play? It is my prayer that every decision you make is based on fearing God's loss and desiring His gain. Would you encourage others to do the same? To do that calls for a top level decision, doesn't it?

8ᵗʰ Inning

Two Catches and Two Throws to Home Plate!'

The first catch and throw from Betty to Jane
The second catch and throw from me to my parents

Have you ever had a bad relationship with someone, and you realized you were as wrong as the other person? You feel guilty and want to make things right, but you don't know how to contact that person. It is important to God to help you get rid of your guilt. Notice how far God went to help Jane clear her conscience about a relationship. Betty, on the other hand, was alert and made a great catch and a super throw that put out the runner, 'guilt', out at home plate.

Then God helped my Dad and Mom make a great catch in Arizona that was hit from Illinois. In both these stories you will see how consistent God is to help us clear our conscience.

Let's begin with Jane. I had just concluded giving a Family Focus USA Seminar in California. I asked if there was anyone who would like to share what the Lord did for them during the week.

Jane came up to the microphone and shared what she learned during the session related to clearing one's conscience. Jane stated that two years ago she received a call from Betty, the former roommate she had in college ten years ago. Betty called to ask her forgiveness for being so immature during those college years. Jane was really surprised to hear from Betty at that time. "Betty asked forgiveness, and I simply said, "Yes, I forgive you. I realize I hadn't asked the Lord or Betty to forgive me for being a rotten roommate myself. I bowed my head during the seminar and asked the Lord to forgive me. The next thing I had to do was ask Betty to forgive me, but I didn't know from where she called. I was relieved in one way, because it's a humbling thing to admit you were wrong. What was I to do? Jon said, 'If the Lord wants you to contact someone you offended, and you don't know where they are, He can make it happen. Simply, purpose to ask and leave it in His hands.'"

"The next morning I received a phone call. I couldn't believe my ears. It was Betty. She said, 'Jane, I'm so glad to hear your voice. I couldn't sleep last night. I kept dreaming about you and wondering if something terrible had happened to you. Is anything wrong? Are you alright?'

I told her, "I'm attending a family seminar, and became convicted about the way I behaved as your roommate. Remember when you called me two years ago, and asked my forgiveness? I should have asked your forgiveness right then, but I wasn't as mature as you at that time. I wanted to do it now, but couldn't, because I didn't know from where you called me two years ago. I can't believe it. Here you are calling me. This is a miracle. From where are you calling me?"

Betty said, 'South Carolina.'

This story shows how the Spirit of God can reach across a continent, and /or around the world, if it will suit His purposes. I titled this short inning 'Hey, Great Catch and

Throw to Home Plate!' because Betty was sensitive enough to 'catch' the nudging of the Holy Spirit and to make that phone call, (to make the 'throw') from South Carolina to Jane's home plate that removed the 'guilt'. Good for you Betty! Good for you Jane. You both complied with what is found in Acts 24:16 ..... "I myself always strive to have a conscience without offense toward God and men." (NKJV)

Jane asked the Lord to forgive her, and then He set it up for Jane to ask Betty's forgiveness. That was a bold thing for her to confess that night in front of all those people The Lord was truly glorified through her testimony.

Is your conscience clear? You cannot make consistent right decisions when you have a guilty conscience. Purpose in your heart to clear your conscience and God will get the play in motion.

Isn't this a great game?

My parents caught what I threw from Illinois to Arizona

God can speak through the mouths of babes; therefore, let's see how He used me, as a baby Christian, after this baby blew it royal. It's worth my having to limp and to share my humiliation to encourage you with the wonderful results the Lord brought about for His glory.

Dad and Mom retired and moved to Arizona. Bev and I raised our family in Illinois. God helped my Dad and Mom make a great catch two years after they saw me make a huge error on the field in a previous inning. That great catch won the game for them. Read on and watch this unfold.

Dad and Mom came to visit us in Illinois a little over five years after I had become a Christian. I began sharing with them what Jesus had been doing in my life. I was enthused about my new found faith, and yet my Dad didn't seem to know what I was talking about. Get ready – here comes my huge error.

I said, "Dad? Do you love me?"

Dad said, "Sure! Why do you ask?"

I said, because you never told me the most important thing a guy could know."

He said, "What's that?" I answered, "You never told me how I could know where I'm going when I die. Why didn't you tell me Dad? I could have been killed and gone to hell if I hadn't heard the answer from General Harrison who spoke at a banquet that Bev and I attended." I paused and Dad said, "I didn't tell you because I didn't know."

I felt sick inside. I figured Dad knew everything. Dads are supposed to know everything, especially about something as important as this. Right?

Then Dad said something that made me see that his background had not been the best as far as understanding from a Biblical perspective.

He said, "I will not believe in, or follow, a God who will cast people into hell."

I said, "Dad, you have to climb over a mountain of Bibles, a mountain of Scripture tracts, and churches; over a mountain of people who have prayed for you, evangelical radio programs, and television crusades. On the last mountain, you climb you'll have to walk right past the cross. If you do that, you did it yourself. That's how hard God made it for us to go to hell."

I had been coming on too strong, and I saw my audience slip away rather quickly. Mom came in, having heard me spout off, and she said, "Reuben, let's go home." Dad and Mom got in their car, and headed for home in Arizona that very hour. I was still upset that Dad hadn't been the one to explain to me the most important thing I should know while I was growing up under his roof.

The Lord dealt with me in a loving way right after I had been so unloving to my own Dad. He reminded me what Dad had said and why Dad had looked at life the way he did. When my Dad was growing up he had been subjected to Eastern religions, which consisted of moving up different levels toward god by doing good deeds. He had been involved with different cults trying to fill the void in his heart.

Bev knew I was really bothered by how I had talked to Dad. She had been telling me about a seminar on basic youth conflicts that a man named Bill Gothard conducted in Chicago, Illinois. For two years she thought I needed something more, especially since I didn't know how to deal with my own Dad in the proper way.

I didn't hear from Dad or Mom for two years. I didn't know what to do. I was still an immature Christian, but my wife saw how much the Lord was changing me, so one day, she said, "Jon, there is another Bill Gothard seminar in Chicago that teaches about the basic youth conflicts. You work with teens. Let's go to hear what Bill has to say"

The Lord started working on me because He knew the time was right for me to have a growth spurt spiritually. We attended our first seminar that fall of 1969. One of the things that Bill said pertained to my Dad and Mom. He said, "Have you ever sent a thank you letter to your Dad and Mom for raising you? God wrote a love letter from heaven, we call the Bible. I'm glad He did. Your parents will welcome a love letter from you in appreciation for all they have done for you."

My heart leaped. I wanted to do that! Then the Lord reminded me of something else that I had known but had put on the shelf. My Dad and Mom's first-born son died when he was five years old. They were so torn by this loss that they swore that if they ever had another child they would never allow themselves to get close to that child for fear of more pain if that child died.

Now here is where the game really gets interesting. My Dad and Mom had been in the stands watching me play the game of life. They saw me witnessing too strongly and that was the huge error I made two years before in the most agonizing inning of my life. They left the ballpark. Again, God uses everything for His own use and glory. He was about to help me correct my error by showing me the proper way to make a play that could be noticed even in Arizona. The following is the letter I sent them:

Dear Dad and Mom,

I made a huge error in coming across like a pious punk in our home, while you were visiting us two years ago. I want to thank you Mom for carrying my twin sister and me for nine months. Thank you for what you went through; the labor pains and all. I so admire you and thank you for feeding, bathing and clothing us. You always worked hard to keep the house clean for us. I feel badly that I hurt you when I spoke out of turn to Dad. Mom, I was wrong. Will you forgive me?

Dad, you and Mom are the best parents in the world for me. God handpicked you to raise Bob, Bill, Yvonne and me. Thank you for working such long hours stocking grocery shelves until one and two in the morning, so we would have food on the table, clothes on our back and a roof over our heads. Thank you for not moving to Texas, when you had a chance to be promoted, so I could finish college at Bradley. If we had moved, I might not have signed with the Orioles. You and Mom sacrificed more than I will ever know, and I love you for it. Dad, I was wrong for the way I treated you. You didn't fail me. I failed you. Can you find it in your heart to forgive me?

I love you both, and I want to spend eternity with you in heaven. The only way I know how to get to heaven is to do what Jesus said, and that was for me

*to receive Him into my life as my Savior and Lord.
Dad and Mom, He has changed my life for the better,
and He is the one who helped me write this. You and
Mom are God's best choice of parents for me. I love
you, and I hope this letter finds you in good health.*

*Your appreciative and loving son,
Jon*

Dad and Mom called me two days after I mailed that letter. This call was the first contact they initiated in two years after my insensitive remarks to Dad. Dad said, "Hi, Jon. Your mother and I are on this phone together. Would you get Bev; we have something to say." Bev got on the phone and Dad said, "Thank you for your letter, Jon." In unison they said, "Jesus Christ is now our Savior and Lord."

I'll never forget those beautiful words from my Dad and Mom. It gets to me every time I tell this story, and even now as I type this out for you to read. From then on they supported our ministry. Bev and I heard them make that 'great catch' right over the phone. The letter that God helped me write was like a heavenly contract from God for them to sign.

Now, throw those crutches away, Jon. You don't have to limp anymore. God gives power to the humble.

God wanted my parents on His team. God didn't care how old they were. He helped them make that great catch; receiving His Son Jesus into their lives. Now they are on the team, qualified by Jesus, who took their place on the cross and gave them His uniform of righteousness. Several years later the Lord took them home to be with Him in heaven. We are so happy to know that they are both in heaven today.

I hope you made the great catch during this inning. If you are still in the stands, be sure to have your glove ready. The Bible states in II Pet. 3:9 "The Lord is not slack concerning His promise, as some count slackness, but is longsuffering toward us, not willing that any should perish but that all should come to repentance."(NKJV)

If you haven't yet said, "Jesus, come into my heart and wash my sins away. I receive you as my Savior and Lord," I pray that you will. Then you know you have made the great catch. Remember, Christianity is not only taught, it's caught. I'd love to hear from you.

9th Inning

He 'Connected' The First Inning And The Last.

A baseball player has to connect with the ball in order to get a hit. Christians have to have confidence that God can connect our prayer to His answer to give us success every inning we play for the Lord. A 'baseball' is used in the ballpark to make that game function. In God's game of life He uses 'faith' to make Christianity function. He says in Heb 11:6 "But without faith it is impossible to please Him." (NKJV)" We can't connect without it. If there is no connection the game is flat.

We know how to find a baseball. Where do we look for faith? The Bible says to ask Him. We see in James 1:5-8 "If you want to know what God wants you to do, ask him, and he will gladly tell you, for he is always ready to give a bountiful supply of wisdom to all who ask him; he will not resent it. But when you ask him, be sure that you really expect him to tell you, for a doubtful mind will be as unsettled as a wave of the sea that is driven and tossed by the wind; and every decision you then make will be uncertain, as you turn first this way and then that. If you don't ask with faith, don't expect the Lord to give you any solid answer." (TLB)

There's that word faith again. Where do we find this ball of faith needed to play this game of life? I asked God and He sent me right back to the very first verse of this same chapter. Heb 11:1 "Now faith is the substance of things hoped for, the evidence of things not seen." (NKJV)

My friend, Bob, gave a great physical illustration of this spiritual truth. First, he asked me to look at this verse and in particular the words hoped for. He said, "The words, hoped for, could be used to represent prayer. He raised his left hand, fingers up with the heel of his hand facing me. Next, he said, "The word, evidence, could represent the answer to that prayer." He put up his right hand, fingers up with the heel of his hand facing me. The palms of his hands were facing each other about a pencil length apart.

As he was standing there in that position, he took a pencil and placed it in a horizontal position between the palms of both hands. He said, "The pencil acts as the connector between the prayer and the answer, represented by my two hands. Now, let the pencil represent faith. So, as the pencil connects the two hands, faith connects the prayer to the answer."

I thought, "Is faith the only way to get from the prayer to the answer? Couldn't my praying a lot get me to the answer? No. For the Bible says in Rom 14:23, "for whatever *is* not from faith is sin." (NKJV)

I asked myself, "Since faith is the only thing that God honors to get to the answer, where do I get this faith to fill the gap? After all, I want to please God."

We live in a world where people use faith every day. A young man asked me how the world exhibits faith. I said, "I noticed when you came into my office, you didn't check out the chair before you sat down. That's faith in a chair you assumed would not collapse.

You exhibited faith when drove your car here today. You had to believe that the cars speeding toward you would stay on their side to the road, or you wouldn't be here in the first place." He agreed.

Can you use that kind of faith to please God? No. The Bible has the answer in Rom 10:17, "So then faith *comes* by hearing, and hearing by the word of God." (NKJV) The faith that pleases God must come from His Word, not from the everyday faith we exhibit when we sit down in a chair or drive a car. Look what our present tense position is the moment we trust in Jesus as our Savior and Lord. Eph 2:6 "and raised us up together, and made us sit together in the heavenly places in Christ Jesus."

We ask, "Why is God only pleased by the faith that comes from His word?" We find in John 1:1 "In the beginning was the Word, and the Word was with God, and the Word was God. Verse 14, And the Word became flesh, and dwelt among us," (NKJV)

The Old Testament people cried out to God. "Send us word." This verse states that God sent His Word in the flesh. He sent His Son Jesus in answer to their cry. Therefore, faith comes from reading the Word, and Jesus is the Word made flesh. The Bible says in Matt. 3:17 "This is my beloved Son, in whom I am well pleased." (NKJV)

I get it. Faith is the only thing that pleases the Father because Jesus is the substance (in the flesh) that connects the prayer to the answer. He is the connector. He is the solid pencil that connects the two hands in Bob's illustration. It isn't my praying a lot that connects the prayer to the answer. Jesus is the only One who can connect the prayer to the answer that pleases His Father. The connection is not some mystical mist. It's a solid connection that establishes peace and confidence that our prayers will be answered.

Gal. 2:20 states, "I have been crucified with Christ; nevertheless, I live, Yet not I, but Christ lives in me and the life I now live in the flesh, I live by the faith of the Son of God, who loved me and gave Himself for me." (KJV) In other words, it's the Lord's confidence in Himself that connects the prayer to the answer. We get faith through reading about Jesus in His word. God honors His Word. The Word and Jesus are one in the same. Faith and Jesus are like one in the same as far as what pleases God.

The Bible shows us something that is very humbling. Look at Rom 8:26-27 "And in the same way — by our faith — the Holy Spirit helps us with our daily problems and in our praying. For we don't even know what we should pray for nor how to pray as we should, but the Holy Spirit prays for us with such feeling that it cannot be expressed in words. And the Father who knows all hearts knows, of course, what the Spirit is saying as He pleads for us in harmony with God's own will." (TLB)

In other words, we give our best shot when we pray, and the Holy Spirit fills in the gap and shares with the Father what we really need. The Holy Spirit makes our prayers complete. This doesn't mean we should be haphazard about praying. We pray, and the Holy Spirit takes it from there.

We are to have confidence in His confidence in Himself to connect the prayer to the answer and here is another reason for this belief. Heb. 12:2 "looking unto Jesus, the author and finisher of our faith," (NKJV)

Jesus authored the confidence. He has confidence in Himself, and He is the finisher of our confidence in Him. Look what it says in John 15:5b... "For apart from me you can't do a thing." (NKJV)

"It's all about Jesus. He did it all. Our joy comes from being obedient to Him. Reading the "Word" and having Jesus in my heart guarantees me the faith that pleases God.

Isn't this great news? Are you reading the Bible every day? If not, let me ask a silly question. Do you eat food every day? The more you read the Bible the greater will be your confidence that Jesus connects the prayer to the answer. Jesus and faith are like one in the same. Both Jesus, and faith that comes from Jesus, pleases the Father. If you don't eat every day you could become malnourished. The spiritual food is right there. As the Lord said, "Take and eat."

10ᵗʰ Inning

Three 'Catches' In Three Different Innings

Guess What? This game is going "Extra Innings".

My first book, 'The Winning Pitch', tells how many different people came to know Jesus Christ as their Savior and Lord. This inning captures the unique way the Lord made Himself real to our children, Lee, Mark and Holly. Christianity is not only taught; it's caught. I hope these three stories encourage you and your loved ones that God loves us and is not willing that any should perish.

Lee was our first-born. He experienced many things first so that Mark and Holly had the chance to go to school on how slowly, or quickly he learned. When they saw him succeed, they knew what they could do to succeed as well. When Lee failed, they knew what to avoid. As it says in the Old Testament, we have a choice of what we want chasing us. We see in Proverbs 13:21."Curses chase sinners, while blessings chase the righteous!" (TLB)

Lee, at the ripe old age of five, was watching Billy Graham on one of his televised crusades. Since I was not home that evening Bev told me, "I was really into what

Billy was saying during his message and near the end of the program the people began walking forward to where Billy was standing. I didn't know if Lee was old enough to understand what Billy was saying until Lee asked, ' Mom, why are those people going up there?' I said, "They are walking up there to show that they asked Jesus into their hearts."

Lee didn't say a word, but I noticed that he bowed his head.

After a moment he looked up and asked, "Do you know what I just did?'

I said, "No Lee. What did you do?"

He said, with a big smile on his face, "I asked Jesus to come into my heart."

We were as happy as we could be, especially since we didn't understand salvation for ourselves until **after** we were married. We noticed a big change in Lee's attitude right away.

He began to have concerns for his siblings Mark and Holly which he didn't before. We prayed with him, told him Bible stories, and talked to him about how we had become Christians, along with what Jesus was doing in our lives.

Two years later, when Lee was seven years old, we were sitting at the dinner table and Lee looked at me and said, "Dad, I'm not sure if Mark is a Christian. Mark was now five years old.

I said to Lee, "Ask Mark if he is a Christian."

Lee turned to Mark and said, "Hey Mark. Are you a Christian?"

Mark kept stuffing food into his mouth and said, "I don't know."

Lee turned to me and said, "Dad, Mark doesn't know if he is a Christian."

I told Lee to ask Mark if he would like to become a Christian."

Lee turned to Mark and asked, "Mark, do you want to be a Christian?"

Mark, chewing his food said, "I don't know."

Lee said, "Dad, Mark doesn't know if he wants to be a Christian or not."

I said, "Lee, ask Mark if he would like to go to heaven when he dies."

Lee asked, "Mark do you want to go to heaven when you die?"

Mark said, "I don't know."

Lee turned to me again and said. Mark doesn't know if he wants to go to heaven."

I said, "Ask Mark if he wants to go to hell."

Lee said, with compassion in his voice, "Mark do you want to go to hell?"

Mark yelled out, "No way!!"

Lee said, "Dad, Mark doesn't want to go to hell."

That was a fascinating experience watching the exchange between Lee and his little brother and me. Then Lee and I went through the gospel with Mark. The whole family watched Mark ask Jesus to come into his heart. Holly observed what was going on, but she was only two years old at the time. There would come a time for her to hear the good news so she could make her own decision. We had no idea how soon that presentation to her would be.

Soon after Mark's conversion at the dinner table, Bev was walking down the hall, and she heard Mark yelling at Holly to get on her knees. Bev looked into the bedroom, and Mark was pushing down on the shoulders of his two-year-old sister trying to get her on her knees. While He was pressing on her, he kept saying, "Get on your knees Holly, you're going to heaven with me!" Holly yelled back, "I don't want to!"

Holly must have thought Mark was going to heaven right then. Mark had seen us on our knees when we prayed so he thought this had to be the right thing to do. One thing Holly knew for sure, Mark was not going to get her on her knees. As far as Mark was concerned, he was going to heaven and Holly was going with him. Over the years Mark has not lost his evangelical vigor, except to say that he has learned to be a tad more diplomatic.

As Holly grew, she showed the normal signs of not being a Christian. She learned that when you make wrong choices, consequences follow. Natural consequences are used of God to get our attention; to show us our need for Him. We watched the Lord lovingly draw Holly to Himself from the time Mark enthusiastically tried to help God out until she was five years old. Holly was in trouble again and Bev felt led to have Holly pray the sinner's prayer of salvation. We still saw little evidence of Holly's spirit changing. She continued to do her own thing such as walking across the street without first looking left or right. The Lord gave us many ideas as to how we could curb Holly's determination. As they say in baseball, we benched her.

When Holly was seven, she was sitting on a chair for not obeying. She didn't have to read anything, but if she wanted to read, she could only read a Bible picture book, or The Living Proverbs, a separate booklet from The Living Bible. We know that the book of Proverbs can help deal with every situation one could experience in a lifetime. While Holly sat there reading one day, she came across an alarming verse. She was not to get off the chair or her time to sit would be extended, but could not contain herself. She had to get up and show her Mom what God said about her rebellious attitude. Holly read in Proverbs 15:9 "The Lord despises the deeds of the wicked but loves those who try to be good. If they stop trying, the Lord will punish them; if they rebel against that punishment, they will die." (TLB)

Holly said, "Mom, look what the Bible says about how I've been acting. That won't happen to me will it, Mom?"

Bev said, "Holly, God loves you, and will use the mistakes you make to show you that you really need Him in your heart to empower you to do what's right. He has already done what He could to show you that He loves you. He took your sins upon Himself so you wouldn't have to die on the cross for your own sins. That's love, Holly."

A few weeks after the talk Holly had with her mom, she was in trouble at school. That very next weekend she initiated trouble during Sunday school and gave her mom a mean look. When we arrived home, I thought it was time to have another chat with Holly.

I said, "Holly, do you have Jesus in your heart?

She said, "No."

I said, "I know you were only two years old when Mark enthusiastically encouraged you to pray for Jesus to come into your heart. Do you remember that, Holly?"

Holly said, "I don't remember."

I said, "Your Mother prayed with you to receive Jesus into your heart when you were five years old. Do you remember that?

Holly said, "I prayed because Mommy wanted me to."

I asked, "Holly, do you like getting into trouble so often? What is going through your mind when you are sitting on the chair for something you did wrong?"

She said, "I sit there and say, 'I'm going to win. I'm going to win.'

I said, "You're in trouble over and over again. Holly, do you think you are winning? You're seven years old Holly. Do you know where you will go when you die?"

She said, "I know it's not heaven."

You don't seem to understand or appreciate what Jesus did for you. Would you like to understand?" She said, "Yes, I want to."

I said, "Good for you. Discipline is tough, isn't it Holly?" She agreed.

What happened next is not something that I recommend to other parents. Since it painted the picture of what scriptures says, I felt led to do the following.

I said, "Holly, I love you, and I'm going to take your discipline for you. Instead of me disciplining you, I'm going to have you discipline me."

She said, "But Daddy, you didn't do anything wrong, I did."

I said, "Holly, Jesus didn't do anything wrong, but He loved you so much that He took your discipline on Himself when He died on the cross for you. Therefore, I'm taking your discipline to show you what Jesus did for you. I love you, Holly."

I lay across the bed and Holly spanked me as described in the Bible. She cried and said, "Daddy, you didn't do wrong, I did." As Holly saw that I loved her so much that I was willing to take her place and received what she knew she deserved, she saw a picture of what Jesus did for her. She stopped, and we hugged.

She experienced the understanding she needed to genuinely give her heart and life to Jesus. She realized and appreciated what Jesus did for her.

I asked Holly if she was ready to ask Jesus into her heart.

She said, "Yes, I'm ready now." Holly initiated one of the most adult prayers I have ever heard. After she thanked Jesus for washing her sins away, she asked Jesus to come into her heart to be her Savior and Lord. Then she threw her arms around Bev and me, and we rejoiced together. Holly had changed. We could see it on her face.

Soon after that we received a call from a Christian teacher at school who had been praying for Holly.

She asked, "What happened to Holly? She is a different girl."

We were thrilled to tell the teacher that Holly put her trust in Jesus Christ.

The teacher said, "I could tell! What a difference."

We thanked the teacher for praying for Holly and for being a good Christian example to her.

We thank the Lord for our three children and for God showing them that Christianity is catching. It's caught as well as taught. God knew what inning Holly would make that fantastic catch.

If you are the Dad, the Mom or the child this inning, you were hand picked by God to be the best at the position you're playing right now. He will change your position right on through the line up as the game goes on. Do you think you're playing the best you can in your position right now? Ask the Coach. Ask the other players. They will gladly tell you. God gives power to the humble.

If you see that you're not on God's team, and you want to be, do what we did. Ask Jesus into your heart right now. Here is a great prayer: Claim it as though you wrote it out yourself.

"Lord Jesus, I need You. Thank You for dying on the cross for my sins. I open the door of my life and receive You as my Savior and Lord. Thank you for forgiving my sins and giving me eternal life. Take control of the throne of my life. Make me the kind of person you want me to be."

Here is how to know that Christ is in your life:

Did you receive Christ into your life? Then, where is He? He said He would come in. Would He mislead you? No. You can count on the trustworthiness of God Himself and His Word.

The Bible promises eternal life to all who receive Him. It says in I John 5:11-13 "And this is the testimony: that God has given us eternal life, and this life is in His Son. He who has the Son has life; he who does not have the Son of God does not have life. These things I have written to you who believe in the name of the Son of God, that you may know that you have eternal life,"

If you prayed that prayer, let me know. My phone number is in the back of this book along with my e-mail address I would love to hear from you.

11ᵗʰ Inning

Amanda Played 3 ½ Innings

For years now, Amanda's outstanding performance continues to draw others to join the team.

Amanda, our granddaughter, learned how to play the game of life well in the first three and one half years of her life. Those few years combine some of the most tremendous blessings and excruciating heartaches I ever experienced. Humanly, we tend to praise and question God at the same time when God takes a great player out of the line up. When you are blessed it's fantastic. When you're in pain like this you just don't know what to think. If there was ever a time I needed to talk with God, it was during the last few weeks of Amanda's life. I had to get with Him often because I didn't know how to help anyone else on the family team. None of us could help each other the way we wanted to.

Our children, Lee, Mark, Holly and their mates have all raised wonderful children and a few have already graduated from high school.

Amanda showed amazing talent as she learned the game of life at a very young age. Lee and Terry Burnham, her parents, are very proud of Amanda. In fact, I am typing this story about Amanda on what would have been her 26th birthday, May 24th, 2007. Watch how this young grand-daughter, at the age of three and a half, was used of God to bring many people to Christ for salvation.

One evening Amanda and her mom, Terry were at Grandma and Grandpa Burnham's home watching television. Soon it was time to watch Billy Graham during one of his many evangelistic crusades. We were talking when the music ended, and Billy began to preach. When he was finished, he called for the people in the audience, who had just prayed to receive Christ, to come forward to show 'publicly' what they had done.

As the people were going forward Amanda asked the same question that her dad, Lee, had asked his Mom when he was watching a Billy Graham Crusade at the age of five. Amanda said, "Grandma, why are those people going up there?" Bev said, "While they were listening to Billy Graham, they asked Jesus to come into their hearts. They are going up there to show that they did that." Amanda listened to her grandma, but didn't say anything until she arrived home.

When they reached home Amanda asked, "Mommy, where is Jesus?"

Terry said, "He's everywhere, and He wants to live in our hearts. Amanda, do you know what sin is?"

Amanda said, "Yes. It's when you tell me to do something, and I turn my head and stick out my tongue."

Terry asked, "How does that make you feel?"

Amanda answered, "All yucky inside."

Terry said, "Jesus wants to come into your heart and clean out that yucky feeling. Do you want to pray and ask Jesus to come into your heart?"

Amanda said, "Yes, but I don't know how?"

Terry said, "I'll help you. Say this; "Lord Jesus.""

Amanda said, "Lord Jesus."

Terry continued, "Forgive my sins."

On her own Amanda said, "Forgive my sins and come into my heart." Amanda looked up with an expression that declared that she knew what she had done.

The next morning, Terry wanted to make sure that Amanda understood what she had done the previous night, so she asked, "Amanda, did anything happen yesterday that you want to tell Daddy?" Amanda stumbled around the bed to get right in her Daddy's face and said, "I axed Jesus in my heart." Lee was thrilled. He found out later that Amanda had asked her Grandma the same question he had asked his Mom while watching Billy Graham on TV.

I mentioned that Amanda stumbled around the bed to talk to her daddy. Lee and Terry had noticed that she was not as stable on her feet as she had been. They had a doctor's appointment to have her checked.

At the doctor's office, they were instructed to go to the hospital for an MRI to see what is going on inside Amanda's head that was causing her to stumble. The MRI showed that there was a tumor attached to her brain stem that had to be removed surgically.

While waiting for surgery, they had to keep Amanda out of Sunday school for fear she would get a cold that would postpone the surgery. Sunday morning, Lee was reading Bible stories and singing to Amanda. Lee, looked at Amanda, and asked, "Do you know what Mommy and Daddy want more than anything in the world?"

Amanda said, "No Daddy, what?"

Lee said, "We want you to live for Jesus the rest of your life."

Amanda looked a little puzzled, and she said, "Well, I axed Him in." In other words, won't that follow?

A short time later Amanda was in the hospital the night before the operation was to take place. In the same room with Amanda was a six-year-old girl who had already been operated on, and she was eating some Jell-O.

While Bev and I sat on Amanda's hospital bed, she was having the best time putting little cartoon stickers on our faces. Then, all of a sudden, she slid off her bed and climbed up on the bed of the six-year-old girl. She was right in her face and began to sing, "Jesus loves me this, I know, for the Bible tells me so…" She sang all she could remember of that song. Her Aunt Holly, also in the room, stepped forward and asked Amanda if she would like to sing, "Tell the world that Jesus loves you………." Both Holly and Amanda sang that song to this little girl. As they sang those songs I noticed that Amanda kept looking over her shoulder at me with a look on her face that said, "Grandpa, I don't think she's one of us. I don't think she knows my Jesus." I will never forget the look of concern Amanda showed for her six year old roommate. Here she was, not knowing the seriousness of her own upcoming operation, witnessing to this girl in song.

The nest day Amanda was operated on. During surgery she had to be resuscitated three times as the surgeon was removing the tumor which had grown onto her brain stem. She came out of the surgery all right, but soon she lapsed into a coma that lasted several days. Then she saw Jesus, the very one she had asked into her heart such a short time before. I remember after Amanda had asked Jesus to come into her heart, she asked Bev, "Grandma, when I go to heaven will Jesus hold me?"

We're sure Jesus held her.

The doctor asked Lee and Terry to come into his office. He shook his head slightly from side to side indicating that Amanda didn't come out of the coma, and that her brain wave was flat. Lee and Terry stood and hugged the doctor. They said, "You did all you could. Amanda is in heaven."

It was Valentine's Day when the Lord took Amanda home. We are so proud of Lee and Terry. They had given themselves to the Lord years ago, and they dedicated Amanda to the Lord when she was born. From then on Amanda was

God's little girl. God gave Amanda to Lee and Terry for a few brief years, and then He took her home.

Bev and I could not identify with Lee and Terry, since we had never lost a child. Only those who have lost a child could really understand and identify with Lee and Terry. We thank the Lord for another couple, Tom and Sue Allen, who had lost a child. They came alongside Lee and Terry as none of us could. What a mature Christian thing to do. Tom and Sue ministered to Lee and Terry, and then they all ministered to others who had a similar experience of loss in their lives.

How could I ever help my son? I could not identify with him. He could not identify with me either. Months later, Lee called me to get together with him. He said, "Dad, I will never be the same. Part of me is gone. I know I will see her again. I'm happy for her, but I miss her. Dad, when I think about her it hurts so badly I have to put her out of my mind. Then I feel guilty for being disloyal by not thinking about her."

I prayed silently that God would give me something from His word to help my son. I was sure He knew what to say. The Lord's thoughts caused me to ask Lee, "If you wanted to have someone get an answer to his prayer, who would you pick?"

Lee said, without hesitation, "Jesus!"

We turned to His prayer in John 17:23-24 "I in them and You in Me, all being perfected into one – so that the world will know You sent me and will understand that You love them (Amanda) as much as you love Me. Father, I want them (Amanda) with me –..."(TLB) Jesus did get an answer to His prayer.

I continued, "Lee, that verse also says, "Father, I want the world to know that You love Lee as much as you love me." One day Jesus will get an answer to His prayer, and God will bring you home to be with Him and Amanda."

I asked Lee to recall a verse in Eph. 2:6 "And lifted us up from the grave into glory along with Christ, where we sit with Him in the heavenly realms – all because of what Christ Jesus did." (TLB) This is a present tense statement for all Christians. Our position is there, right now. Viewing things from up there, sitting with the Father, the Son and the Holy Spirit, gives us a better view than we have down here.

I added, "Could it be that God knew that more people would come to Him by taking Amanda home when she was only three and a half than if she lived to be one hundred? That's a way to try to look at life from God's point of view. I don't really know what to say. I'm just trying to comfort you as best I can. I feel so helpless trying to help."

"Lee said, "Thanks Dad. I believe what you're saying. It's nobody's fault. God knows what he's doing, but it still hurts."

I told Lee, "Your Mom, and I haven't lost a child, so we don't pretend to understand what you are going through. Along with experiencing the loss of Amanda, we have a son who has just lost his child, and we don't know what to do to comfort him. I thought I'd never stop crying. We know the Lord will give His comfort to us all through His grace and mercy. We are just hanging in there with you, Lee. We love you and Terry very much."

Being Lee's Dad, I get choked up as I type this, but I wanted the reader to be blessed by Amanda's short life here on earth. What happened the first month after she went home to heaven? I personally know of thirty people who trusted Jesus Christ as their Savior. Amanda won the game the Lord had her play.

Bev and I were telling Amanda's story on our weekly radio program when we received word, a few days later, that an eight year old gal had listened to the program with her Mom. She said, " Mom, I want to do what that little girl did." Her Mom called and told us that her daughter had received

Jesus into her heart just like Amanda had done. That eight-year-old girl went on to become a godly young woman, and an excellent pianist for the Lord.

Do you know of someone you think might need or want to read this story? That's the way Amanda's story lives on through people like you.

As you watched these innings unfold were you encouraged with how God, the Coach, called the plays? It is all about Him, isn't it? Amanda played only three and a half years, but God used her to draw many others to join the team to play this game of life. Now they're on the team because of how God use Amanda, in the position she played. None of us knows how long the Lord will keep us in the line up. We know that He is the best Coach we will ever have to draw out of us our best game, no matter what position He's having us play. Play your best. People are watching you just like they watched Amanda. I'm sure Amanda is in heaven cheering us on, for she now knows the end from the beginning.

12th Inning

Three 'Line' Drives

Years ago God placed in my heart the desire to begin a full time ministry to encourage people to join His team and how to play to win this game of life. The three line drives refer to three different air<u>line</u> hostesses that God used to put this inning together. His winning game plan becomes evident and brings Him glory.

The first airline hostess is Edith. She and her husband Bud, were used of God to get me into the game full time. They sparked the realization that now is the time, and they got the ball rolling. The second airline hostess is Sally. God used her to encourage me that we are a team, and we need support from one another. Janet, the third airline hostess was on the other team. God gave me the opportunity to show Janet who her coach was and why she should join our team. Her coach did everything he could to keep her from making that decision.

After a short time in baseball with the Baltimore Oriole Organization, I owned and operated a dry cleaning business batting cleanup for 20 years. Then, for the next three and one half years I transitioned into running from one base to another in the real estate business. Watch how this inning developed as God placed me in one position after another until His victorious game plan became a reality when our full time ministry was born.

The First 'Line' Drive

Edith, the first airline hostess, called me to list their house. As I was measuring the rooms I asked Edith why she wanted to sell their house. Edith answered, "Bud and I are getting a divorce."

I told her I would research the comparable homes in the area to establish a market value, and they could look over the listing contract and sign it when I returned that evening.

When I returned Bud met me at the door and ushered me in the dinning room table where Edith was waiting. I started the conversation by asking Bud why they were listing the house.

Edith looked at me as if to say, "Hey, 'dumb dumb', I told you this morning that we're getting a divorce."

I ignored her look of shock because I wanted to see what Bud would say.

He said, "She wants a divorce."

Now I knew which one wanted the divorce.

I looked at Bud and asked him if I could take off my hat.

He said, "What hat?"

I said, "My real estate hat."

He asked, "Why?"

I stated that I would prefer to put on my other hat.

He asked, "What other hat?"

I said, "My marriage counselor hat." I went on to say that I had six different couples in my real estate office that week seeking marriage counseling. I would rather see your marriage salvaged than make money from listing and selling your house. Are you both open to counsel?"

They gave each other a short glance as Bud pulled out his billfold. He took out an old tattered business card of mine and laid it next to my new card on the kitchen table. He looked at me as though a light went on and said, "You're Jon Burnham. I was told to call you six months ago, but I heard that you were a million dollar seller in real estate, so I figured that you would be too busy to talk to me."

My heart sank. My whole purpose for getting into real estate business was be able to make a quick and easy transition into a full time ministry when the Lord gave us the nod. Here I was, sitting across from a man who wanted help with his marriage, but he thought I was too busy. This seemed to make my real estate business counter productive in starting a full ministry.

Edith had made up her mind not to work on the marriage. I left their house with a signed listing contract in my hand, but in my chest was an ach. On the way to my car the pressure increased. I took a deep breath and exhaled to get rid of the pressure. I had had angina once before and I thought it returned. I prayed it wasn't serious. Since my wife is a nurse, and we lived close by, I went right home. I jumped out of the car, ran into the house and told Bev the story of what had just happened with the Bud and Edith. Instead of asking her about the pressure in my chest, I asked Bev, "Are you ready to go full time for the Lord." To my surprise she said, "I've been ready for two years." As soon as she said that, the pressure totally left my chest. It was like God had His hand on this whole experience. The pressure never returned.

Bev had been waiting for me to lead one way or the other, in regard to going full time. We know that the Lord usually prepares the wife ahead of the husband to confirm to the husband that God is in this change. We firmly believed the Lord knew that we were both waiting for Him to show us when, where and how to go full time. He made it very clear with this line drive that we couldn't miss.

Within three months, Bev and I had contacted people interested in helping us go into the ministry. We wanted God to send us out by the body of believers to make sure we were not doing this on our own. We had given two Family Focus USA Seminars in a local church, and the leadership there said, "We know that God's hand is on your ministry. We want to give you free office space so that people can come and hear what the Lord would have them do as you counsel through His word." Bev and I were ecstatic with this generous good news. We thanked God for men like that. We wanted the body of believers, known in the Bible as the Church, to support this ministry as we served Him.

We had three criteria that would show us that the Lord was truly in our ministry.

One: The Lord would send the people for counsel.
Two: People would trust Jesus as their Savior and Lord.
Three: The Lord would supply our needs financially.

God led us 'not' to charge a set fee for our counsel. We wanted to trust God to support us through 'gifts and donations' from the people we counseled and from others who wanted this ministry to continue.

Watching this inning develop I see the Lord as the blessed controller of all things and this line drive was no exception. He also helped us make the catch. God used every position he had me play in the past to develop the kind of pitcher He wanted me to be so I would throw His pitches to others through counseling, seminars and our radio ministry. I hope you are having special innings loaded with God's blessings as you play by His game plan.

The Second 'Line' Drive

Sally, a Christian air<u>line</u> hostess, watched what was happening and began to pray when she saw me talking to Anna, a pilot's wife. It was later confirmed to Sally that I was practicing what I preached in my book, "The Winning Pitch". When you practice what you preach God will fly in some teammates to back you up with prayer.

I was sitting on the plane waiting for it to take off for Texas. I was to meet our publicity agent to promote the first book I wrote, "The Winning Pitch". Just before we took off I noticed that the plane was full, yet there was a vacant seat next me. At the last minute Anna, a young woman in her thirties, sat down next to me. Anna introduced herself as the wife of one of the pilots flying the plane.

When the roar of the engines settled down after take off, I picked up my book and began reading. I wrote it, so why am I reading it? Since I was going to be interviewed in Texas on Family Net, a Christian Cable network, I was reviewing my book anticipating questions they might ask.

Anna leaned over and asked what I was reading.

I told her that I had written this book and was to be interviewed in Texas. I told her that the program would be seen all over the country.

She asked me what the book was about.

I gave her the short version of how I became a Christian from having been an egotistical foul-mouthed baseball pitcher in the Baltimore Oriole Organization.

I asked Anna if she and her husband liked baseball. Anna said they loved baseball.

The noise level on this plane was still too high to talk in a normal conversational tone so I had to lean way over her way, and she leaned my way. To be heard I had to talk right in her ear. Anna asked me to tell her more about the book. Since this would have taken several minutes, I thought it best to show her the Four Spiritual Laws produced by Campus Crusade for Christ. I learned how to share my faith at their headquarters. This booklet is a great tool that makes salvation very clear.

I handed her The Four Spiritual Laws booklet and told her that my book was filled with stories related to those spiritual laws. I asked her to read it page by page and to let me know if she had any questions. Anna began to read very slowly and with great interest. I was impressed that she was so diligent since some people, when they see that The Four Spiritual Laws are about God, leaf though it so fast that you would assume they were speed readers.

The following is what Anna read:

* From *Have You Heard of the Four Spiritual Laws?* by Bill Bright © Copyright 1966- 2008 Campus Crusade for Christ and Bright Media Foundation. All rights reserved. <u>Used by permission</u>

Just as there are physical laws that govern the physical universe, so are there are spiritual laws that govern your relationship with God.

LAW 1

God **loves** you and offers a wonderful plan for your life.

God's Love

"God so loved the world that He gave His one and only Son, that whoever believes in Him shall not perish but have eternal Life" (John 3:16, NIV).

God's Plan

[Christ speaking] "I came that they might have life, and might have it abundantly" [that it might be full and meaningful] (John 10:10,).

Why is it that most people are not experiencing the abundant life?

Because…………..

LAW 2

Man is **sinful** and **separated** from God. Therefore, he cannot know and experience God's love and plan for his life.

Man Is Sinful

"All have sinned and fall short of the glory of God" (Romans 3:23).

Man was created to have fellowship with God; but, because of his own stubborn self-will, he chose to go his own independent way and fellowship with God was broken. This self-will, characterized by an attitude of active rebellion or passive indifference, is an evidence of what the Bible calls sin.

Man Is Separated
"The wages of sin is death" [spiritual separation from God] (Romans 6:23).

This diagram illustrates that God is holy and man is sinful. A great gulf separates the two. The arrows illustrate that man is continually trying to reach God and the abundant life through his own efforts, such as a good life, philosophy, or religion—but he inevitably fails.

The third law explains the only way to bridge this gulf…

LAW 3

Jesus Christ is God's **only** provision for man's sin. Through Him you can know and experience God's love and plan for your life.

He Died In Our Place
"God demonstrates His own love toward us, in that while we were yet sinners, Christ died for us" (Romans 5:8)

He Rose from the Dead
"Christ died for our sins....He was buried...He was raised on the third day, according to the Scriptures... He appeared to Peter, then to the twelve. After that He appeared to more than five hundred..." (I Corinthians 15:3-6).

We Receive Christ Through Personal Invitation
[Christ speaking] "Behold, I stand at the door and knock; if any one hears My voice and opens the door, I will come in to him" (Revelation 3:20).

Receiving Christ involves turning to God from self (repentance) and trusting Christ to come into our lives to forgive our sins and to make us what He wants us to be. Just to agree **intellectually** that Jesus Christ is the Son of God and that He died on the cross for our sins is not enough. Nor is it enough to have an emotional experience. We receive Jesus Christ by **faith**, as an act of the **will**.

These two circles represent two kinds of lives:

Self-Directed Life
S - Self is on the throne
† - Christ is outside the life
● - Interests are directed by self, often resulting in discord and frustration

Christ-Directed Life
† - Christ is in the life and on the throne
S - Self is yielding to Christ
● - Interests are directed by Christ, resulting in harmony with God's plan

Which circle best represents your life?
Which circle would you like to have represent your life?

LAW 4

We must individually receive Jesus Christ as Savior and Lord; then we can know and experience God's love and plan for our lives.

We Must Receive Christ

"As many as received Him, to them He gave the right to become children of God, even to those who believe in His name" (John 1:12).

We Receive Christ Through Faith

"By grace you have been saved through faith: and that not of yourselves, it is the gift of God; not as a result of works that no one should boast" (Ephesians 2:8-9).

When We Receive Christ, We Experience A New Birth

(Read John 3:1-8.)

I answered her questions, and she continued reading until she saw the two circles relating to two different lives. The circle on the left represents one going to hell and the circle on the right represents one going to heaven.

I asked Anna which circle best represented her life.

She said, "The one on the left."

I asked, "Would you like to have the circle on the right represent your life?"

She said, "Yes, I would."

The following explains how you can receive Christ:

You Can Receive Christ Right Now By Faith Through Prayer

(Prayer is talking with the God)
God knows your heart and is not so concerned with your words as He is with the attitude of your heart. The following is a suggested prayer:

I asked Anna if she would read the prayer and tell me if she thought it covered the desire of her heart.

Lord Jesus, I need You. Thank You for dying on the cross for my sin. I open the door of my life and receive You as my Savior and Lord. Thank you for forgiving my sins and giving me eternal life. Take control of the throne of my life. Make me the kind of person You want me to be.

I asked, "Does this prayer express the desire of your heart? If it does, I invite you to pray this prayer right now, and Christ will come into your life, as He promised.
She said, "Yes, it does."
Anna prayed that same prayer to God, and then she looked at me with a big smile on her face and said, "Thank you."
I asked Anna to read the next paragraph, so she could be sure in her mind and heart what just took place.

How to Know That Christ Is In Your Life

Did you receive Christ into your life? She said she did. According to His promise in Revelation 3:20, where is Christ right now in relation to you? Anna said, 'He's in my heart.'

I said, Christ said He would come into your life. Would He mislead you?" She said, "I don't think so." I then said to Anna, "On what authority do you know God has answered your prayer? I had her read the following sentence. (The trustworthiness of God Himself and His Word.) She claimed that sentence as her very own answer.

The Bible Promises Eternal Life to All Who Receive Christ

"God has given us eternal life, and this life is in His Son. He who has the Son has the life; he who does not have the Son of God does not have the life. These things I have written to you who believe in the name of the Son of God, in order that you may **know** that you have eternal life" **(I John 5:11-13)**.

Anna saw what my book, "The Winning Pitch", was all about. She experienced it first hand. Neither of us knew then that her story would be, 'In The Big Inning'.

Sally, one of the airline hostesses on duty, asked me to come with her. I stood up and followed her to her little hostess area on the plane, and she said, "I see what you're doing. When you were sharing your book and your faith with the pilot's wife, I began to pray. I'm a Christian, and I thought I was the only one on this plane." We laughed, and I thanked her for praying and told her the result of her faithfulness. The Lord flew her in for such an occasion as this.

I was scheduled to switch planes in Atlanta before going on to Texas. I made the switch and noticed that this second plane was booked solid just like the first one. Again, there was an empty seat next to me. Finally, just before take off, a young African American woman sat down next to me. She sweetly asked who I was and where I was going. I told her that I had written a book called the The Winning Pitch and was on my way to Texas to promote it on television. To make a similar story short she too was interested, and before the plane landed in Texas, she received Jesus into her heart as her personal Savior and Lord.

When I arrived in Texas, I was met at the airport by the publicity agent and was taken to the TV studio. My interviewer asked if I had had any recent experiences sharing my faith. The Lord knew he was going to ask me that question, as well as the two people He had prepared to receive Him as their Savior on those two airplanes. God's timing is perfect!

The Third 'Line' Drive

Do you have a friend who is on the 'other' team? I have seen God bring many players over to our team, but never quite as dramatically as Janet. Your friend might want to read this, because down deep, he or she can't really be satisfied playing for a coach like that. He doesn't want to lose any of his players, and he'll do anything to keep them.

Max, and his girlfriend Janet, met me in a quiet room off the hotel lobby. Janet is the third airline hostess in this inning, and Max is a Christian businessman. He was in agony watching Janet throw her life away. Max brought her to see me because she had told him some things that threw him for a loop. He didn't know how to get past her resistance to God. Max wanted her to become a Christian so she could look at what she was doing and want to play for our team. Janet, a sharp twenty six year old gal, came only to please Max. She also had a hidden agenda that she will reveal later in the story.

Janet said, "I came in here at the request of my boyfriend, so before you begin, I want you to know that I sleep around, drink, drug, and smoke. Now give me your best shot."

I asked Janet a few questions and began the presentation of the gospel. I used the same Four Spiritual Laws booklet.

When I finished, I asked, "Now, is there any reason why you wouldn't want to ask Jesus to come into your heart?"

Janet straightened up in her chair and presented her hidden agenda as she stuck out her chin and said, "I can't bring myself to do that!! In fact, I feel prevented." She looked over to her boyfriend as if to say to him, 'See, this was a waste of time.'

I asked, "Would you be interested in knowing why you feel prevented?"

To my surprise she said, "Yes."

I picked up my Living Bible Translation and asked Janet to listen to what Jesus told the Pharisees, the super saints back then? She was actually curious; another surprise. When Janet said she felt 'prevented' she didn't know that her statement triggered my memory bank.

I turned to the book of John in the New Testament. I started reading in John 8: 43-45 "Why can't you understand what I am saying? It is because you are 'prevented' from doing so! For you are the children of your father the devil, and you love to do the evil things he does. He was a murderer from the beginning and a hater of truth—there is not an iota of truth in him. When he lies, it is perfectly normal; for he is the father of liars. And so when I tell the truth, you just naturally don't believe it!" (TLB)

Janet said, "Wait a minute!!! Are you telling me that my spiritual father is the Devil?"

I said, "No!"

She said, "You just said that my spiritual father is the devil. I heard you."

As I picked up my Bible and put it in front of Janet I said, "No. God said that."

She looked totally surprised.

I said, "Let me tell you about your spiritual dad. He hates your guts, because you are born in the image of God. If the devil can prevent you from receiving Jesus as your Savior and Lord, he can take you to hell with him when you die. Hey, nice dad. What do you owe a dad like that?"

While he still owned her, Janet said, "I owe him nothing!!"

I looked at her and pointed to heaven and said, "What do you owe God? He sent His own Son to take your place on the cross to shed His blood to wash your sins away, so you won't have to go to hell, but so you can go to heaven when you die. All you need to do is to receive Him into your heart. Now, what do you owe Him?"

Janet bursts into tears and said, "I owe Him my life!"

I asked if she was ready now to trust Jesus to be her Savior and Lord.

She said, "Yes". Janet followed me in prayer. When Janet finished the prayer she stood up, walked over to her boyfriend and said, "I'm going to stop sleeping around, drinking, drugging and smoking."

I asked Janet, "Why are you saying those things?"

Janet turned to me and said, "How can I go on living like that when Jesus died to clean me up so that I could go to heaven? However, Jon, I have a question for you. I came in here with the purpose of putting you down so badly that my boyfriend would not bring me back here to see you or anyone else like you. What happened? I ended up doing the opposite of what I intended."

I answered Janet by saying, "In Romans 10:17 it says, 'faith comes by hearing, hearing by the Word of God.' NKJV

"He created us in such a way that when we hear His Word, faith enters our spirit to enable us to believe what He said. He also created us so that when we hear His Word, we are free to reject it and go our own independent way and suffer the consequences. You chose to use the faith He gave you to receive Him into your heart. Good for you. You could not have made a better choice."

You saw the presentation of the Four Spiritual Laws in this inning. I'm sure the Lord has already orchestrated a game plan for you to use that will help you play your best to glorify God.

If you have a friend on that 'other' team, you can see how the Lord Jesus will be quick to help you draw them over to our team. You saw how He had Sally, a real prayer warrior; fly in to pray for me as I was talking to Anna. God can do the same for you as you share your faith with those on the 'other' team. It's a very sobering thought that if they die, while members of the 'other' team, the Bible says they will go right to hell. That's a great motivation to get them to talk with you and to meet your Coach. Look what Satan, the coach of the 'other' team, did to keep a hold on Janet. Satan couldn't keep her on his team though, could he? Satan has a game plan but our Lord Jesus has already defeated him. Isn't it great to be on the winning team?

The Lord will help you memorize the way to join His team when you get into a conversation with anyone on the other team. If you memorize the plan of salvation it won't sound like a canned speech when you present it. I'm glad I was encouraged to memorize The Four Spiritual Laws. If you want to find out if you are ready to share your faith, get on an airplane and watch what happens.

13ᵗʰ Inning

They 'Waited' and God 'Delivered'

Shellie, Sarah and Andrea 'waited' on Bev and me in three different restaurants, and God 'delivered' what they needed. Many times, I'm in such a hurry, I rush to get in and out of a restaurant, and I miss an opportunity to talk with the waitress. I go in to fill my stomach, while the waitress may have a 'hunger' in her heart. I know how to fill my stomach, but the waitress may not know how and with whom to fill her heart.

His <u>First</u> 'Delivery'

Bev and I were staying in a hotel in Schaumburg, Illinois and we always enjoyed eating in their restaurant. Shellie came up to take our order and she was so friendly we felt right at home. It's our desire, when meeting a new waitress; to look for a natural opening to see what level of interest she or he might have in spiritual things.

Shellie asked what brought us to Schaumburg. We told her that we were here shopping for bargains and other things. Shellie asked, "What other things?"

I said, "To see if there is anyone in this area who might be interested in a bargain we found years ago that's still a bargain today."

She said, "I'm always looking for bargains. What bargain are you talking about?"

I said, "The bargain of going to heaven when you die."

Shellie looked at me like I was from the planet Mars and said, "I don't believe in that stuff."

I asked her what stuff was she talking about.,

She said, "I don't believe in religion."

I replied, "I don't believe in religion either. Religion is our way to reach God. I believe in Christianity; God's way to reach man."

As Shellie whirled away she said, "I'm going to place your order." She stayed away from our table until our order was up. She brought it without a word and didn't come back to fill our glasses of water. Even though Shellie seemed upset, I was glad to see she had convictions about something. She did know what she was against. However, Shellie didn't know the One I was trying to tell her about. I left her a big tip to show that we were not offended by her position on 'religion'.

Several months later we were in the same hotel. We went to their restaurant wondering if Shellie was still there. I had just received my books from the publisher in Florida and brought some of them with me in the car. Bev and I thought it would be good to bring one into the restaurant to see if the next waitress we met was interested in 'bargains and baseball'. Guess what? Shellie came up and greeted us like long lost friends. She may have remembered the tip I left. Shellie also may have remembered how she treated us, but nonetheless she was very pleasant.

As Shellie was taking our order, she saw the book on the table. Bev noticed her observation and jumped right in to say, "Jon wrote a book. He used to be a pitcher in the

Baltimore Oriole Organization." She looked surprised and said she liked baseball. I told her she could have the book. I thought she might throw it away when she discovered it was about the 'bargain'. We finished our meal, and Shellie thanked us for the book. Again, I left her a big tip to let her know that people she thought were 'religious' are not all that bad. We drove home and prayed that the Lord would touch her heart with the stories in my book, <u>The Winning Pitch</u>.

Again, several months later Bev and I were in Schaumburg and stayed at the same hotel. We went in to eat dinner, and there was Shellie. She looked up and saw us coming into the restaurant. She walked right up to us before we sat down and gave Bev and me a big hug. This was amazing. Shellie told us that she didn't know she had to receive Jesus into her heart to be able to understand the things of God. She told us that while reading my book, she stopped and prayed to receive Jesus. Shellie loaned my book to a friend with whom she had been sharing her newfound faith.

We were thrilled with her response to Jesus. On our first visit, she had been against the things of God. Now she was all fired up about Jesus. God's timing is perfect, and this encouraged us even more not to give up on anyone. He did all the changing in her when we were nowhere around. God brings people to Himself as we lift Him up in His rightful place.

We kept in contact with Shellie for months after that. We shared with her about a local church in her area that she might want to attend to help her grow in the Lord. Shellie would call long distance to get our counsel, and we were thrilled with the genuineness of Shellie's conversion to Jesus. She did end up with a real 'bargain' after all.

His <u>Second</u> 'Delivery'

Bev and I were in Galesburg, Illinois and stopped in one of our favorite places to eat. Sarah, the waitress, was very sad. We asked if she was all right, but she seemed distant, so we let it go. One doesn't pick green apples. God can use the natural consequences of life to get out attention.

Before we left the restaurant my wife mentioned that I had been a baseball player. She told us that she and her live in boy friend were really into baseball. Sarah seemed to perk up. We felt free to give her my book hoping they would both read it.

Just two weeks later Sarah called me and began to pour out her problems. It became evident that she wanted to get right with God. She'd read enough of my book to know that God loved her, and she needed to talk about it. Sarah wanted me to step her through the scripture so that she could claim Christ for herself.

After praying on the phone to receive Jesus, she seemed to have a much better attitude. The burden was lifted. Sarah had Jesus as her personal Savior and Lord. What a joy to know that the Lord will reach out to a person right where they are, even on the other end of the phone line. He is in on every phone call we make and every step we take. It's like our friend, Dr. Steve Hauter said in his message one Sunday morning. "Jesus wants to live in your heart. Being in you He's there when you're on the phone, in the kitchen, on the job, in the basement, etc. He can't get any closer than that." Steve was relating the story of Jacob to his congregation. Steve said, "You will find this in Genesis 28:16 "Then Jacob awoke from his sleep and said, "Surely the LORD is in this place, and I did not know it." (NKJV)

God was always there, and all of a sudden Jacob realized that God was right there. Jacob could hardly believe it, since he knew he had lied to his father, robbed his brother and was running away from home. One who is living like that cannot imagine that a Holy God could be anywhere near. One living like that doesn't want God anywhere near. Even if one can imagine Him being very far away, He is right there. God loves you and me just like He loved Jacob. The scripture says in Romans 5:8 "But God demonstrates His own love toward us, in that while we were still sinners, Christ died for us." (NKJV)

Steve went on, "Old Testament or New Testament, the Lord is the same yesterday, today and forever. Here's what it says in the Old Testament about God being everywhere we are. Ps 139:1-18

"O Lord, you have examined my heart and know everything about me. You know when I sit or stand. When far away you know my every thought. You chart the path ahead of me and tell me where to stop and rest. Every moment you know where I am. You know what I am going to say before I even say it. You both precede and follow me and place your hand of blessing on my head. This is too glorious, too wonderful to believe! I can *never* be lost to your Spirit! I can *never* get away from my God! If I go up to heaven, you are there; if I go down to the place of the dead, you are there. If I ride the morning winds to the farthest oceans, even there your hand will guide me, your strength will support me. If I try to hide in the darkness, the night becomes light around me. For even darkness cannot hide from God; to you the night shines as bright as day. Darkness and light are both alike to you. You made all the delicate, inner parts of my body and knit them together in my mother's womb. Thank you for making me so wonderfully complex! It is amazing to think about. Your workmanship is marvelous—and how well I know it. You were there while I was being formed in utter seclusion! You saw me before I was born and scheduled each day of my life before I began to breathe. Every day was recorded in your book! How precious it is, Lord, to realize that you are thinking about me constantly! I can't even count how many times a day your thoughts turn toward me. And when I waken in the morning, you are still thinking of me!" (TLB)

Jesus will set up situations for you to share your faith in Him. I pray that this book helps to motivate you to be ready when He does.

His <u>Third</u> 'Delivery'

Andrea Elser from Peoria, Illinois, gave me permission to tell her story. Many people in the Peoria area have already experienced meeting and being blessed by Andrea.

There are many good restaurants in the Greater Peoria area. We went into a brand new one that became very popular right away, and we believe it was partly due to Andrea.

We were ushered to our seat by the hostess. We sat down and Andrea, a bubbly waitress with personality plus, came to our table to wait on us.

Dan Vonachen, a friend of ours, said hello and talked with us for a few moments as he was on his way to be seated. Andrea must have known Dan because she asked how we knew him. I told her, "Every one in town knows Dan and his dad Pete. I told Andrea I met Dan at church, and he got me into the new chief's baseball park to throw a few pitches to him from the mound. Not too bad for an old man in his sixties to get a chance to pitch a few from the mound in that beautiful ballpark. She said, "You're not in your sixties!" She looked at my wife Bev and said, "He's not in his sixties, is he?" Bev told her I really was. She said, "He sure is a handsome dude for a guy in his sixties." She was well on her way to a nice tip. She went on to ask what beverage we wanted and off she went to get our drinks.

Bev and I smiled at one another for the compliment she had given this old man. She came back with our drinks and said, "Why did you want to throw a ball from the mound at the chief's park?" I told her that I signed with the Baltimore Orioles as a pitcher after graduating from Bradley University. I hadn't thrown a ball from the mound since Dan's dad let me use the mound to do a TV interview promoting my book, The Winning Pitch. I had given Dan and his wife Jennifer my book, and it wasn't long before Bev and I went out to lunch with them. During lunch Dan told me, "I'll get you on the mound at the Chief's ballpark. We'll see if you can still throw the ball sixty feet six inches." What a blast that was as I fired away to Dan at home plate with Bev and Jennifer watching us from the sidelines.

Andrea asked me more about the book I wrote, so I went out to the car and got her one. I signed the book and when I gave it to her, I asked if she would let me know what she thought of it.

A few weeks later I received a letter from Andrea telling me that she had a real love for God, was active in church, and that she loves to read the Bible, but she didn't realize that she needed to receive Jesus Christ into her heart. This was something she hadn't done, so Andrea prayed to receive Jesus to be her Savior and Lord.

This is the same thing that happened to my wife Bev. Bev loved God and was one of the young leaders in her church youth group. It wasn't until Bev was twenty-seven years old that she heard a Bible teacher, Ruby Thompson, say that one must receive Jesus into one's heart. Ruby also said, "Christian means, Christ in one." When Bev heard it put that way it really clicked with her. For it says in John 1:12 "But as many as received Him, to them He gave the right to become children of God, to those who believe in His name:" (NKJV)

Bev received Jesus into her heart by praying a simple prayer admitting that she was a sinner, and that she wanted

Jesus to come into her heart, not to be just another activity, but to be number one.

When Bev shared that with the Andrea, she gave Bev a big hug and said, "I sure admire you". We admire Andrea, our sister in Christ. We have confidence that she will be a bold witness for the Lord Jesus for many years to come.

The following illustration can help a person better understand the personal relationship you can have with God when you receive His Son Jesus as your Savior and Lord:

Before a guy will call a girl for a date, he will have to accept her intellectually, or he won't ask her out in the first place.

Before the girl will accept his invitation, she too will have to intellectually accept him, or she may turn him down. If they intellectually accept one another, they go out and get to know each other a little better. The emotions get going and there must be an acceptance on that level, or he won't keep asking her out, nor will she accept another date with him.

Having accepted her intellectually, and emotionally he may come to the conclusion to willfully spend the rest of his life with her. He has therefore accepted her with his "soul", the intellect, emotion and will, but that does not mean that he's married to her.

She may accept him with her 'soul' in the same way, yet they are not married. They are married when they stand before the authority of a minister, or another similar authority, and exchange marriage vows.

The minister sees this man and woman standing before him, along with the wedding party and all the guests in the audience, and he starts with the man and says, "Do you take this woman to be your lawfully wedded wife, to love, honor and cherish, for richer for poorer, in sickness and in health, for better or for worse, forsaking all others until death parts you?"

The groom could turn to her and say, "Hey sweets, I'll love you the rest of my life, but I can't do this. In fact, I'm out of here." He would then leave the church. However, let's say he chooses to go on with this, and he says, "I do." Notice, that even though he says, "I do", at that point they are not yet married.

The minister turns to the woman and repeats the vows and prompts her to say, "I do." She too could say to the fiancé, "I'll love you the rest of my life, but I can't do this." She would then leave the church. However, let's say she also chooses to go ahead with the ceremony, and she says, "I do."

At this point there is usually an exchange of rings. The ring is a circle, a symbol of eternal love. The minister is free to say, "By the power vested in me from God and by the authority of the state, I now pronounce you husband and wife. Sir, you may kiss the bride."

After the kiss, a discreet way of sealing the marriage, the minister has them face the audience of witnesses to this wonderful event and says, "Ladies and gentlemen, it is my privilege to present to you, Mr. and Mrs. _____."

The people clap; the bride and groom leave for a moment and then return to greet their guests.

How is this a picture of me uniting with Jesus Christ as my Savior and Lord? Let me illustrate:

First of all, God asks His Son, the groom, "Son, have you accepted Jon intellectually?"

Jesus says, "Yes Father, I have."

"The Father says, "But Son, Jon uses your name as a swear word."

Jesus said, "I know Father. Jon is a sinner."

The Father asked Jesus, "Son, have you accepted Jon emotionally?"

Jesus said, "Yes Father, I emotionally and physically took Jon's place on the cross.

God the Father asked, "Son, will you receive Jon into your kingdom?"

Jesus did not walk away two thousand years ago. He said, "I do".

On October 9, 1961 the Father turned to me in the basement of a church on Main street in Washington, Illinois and said, "Jon, intellectually, is Jesus a swear word?"

I said, "No, He is God in the flesh."

God said, "Good. Have you ever gotten emotionally involved with My Son?"

I said, "When I heard that Jesus died on the cross in my place to wash my sins away, I have the emotion of appreciation."

God said, "Will you receive My Son Jesus as your Savior and Lord? Savior means He will save you from Hell, and He will save you for heaven. Lord means boss. This means he will save you from you. Jon, you have been your own worst enemy by being the boss of your own life."

I agreed, for I had been a rotten boss of my own life. I was also in the process of ruining my wife's life. After all, who could run my life better than the One who created me?

So, without further delay I said, "I do".

When I said, "I do" the audience of angels in heaven rejoiced. I was given "Eternal Life".

1John 5:10-13 "He who believes in the Son of God has the witness in himself; he who does not believe God has made Him a liar, because he has not believed the testimony that God has given of His Son. And this is the testimony: that God has given us eternal life and this life is in His Son. He who has the Son has life; he who does not have the Son of God does not have life. These things I have written to you who believe in the name of the Son of God, that you may 'know' that you have eternal life." (NKJV)

All three of these waitresses experienced a great 'delivery' from God, right out of heaven. Each was given eternal life when they said, "I do" to Jesus. They received Jesus Christ as their Savior and Lord.

I hope these real life testimonies and illustrations are encouraging to you, especially when you're hungry in a restaurant where the waitress might be hungry too. She knows you're hungry because you came in to eat. You won't know if she's hungry or not until you take a moment to observe, and perhaps lead out with what the Lord would have you say. He knows she may be hungry, and God will help you hear her hunger pangs. If she growls at you, it's a good thing. You have the food that feeds men's souls. Male waiters get hungry too. I've seen a few of them satisfied with God's Word.

Have the Four Spiritual Laws booklet ready to share with the waitress. If you put it on the table when you leave be sure to slip a nice tip in the pages so she will be more apt to read it.

14th Inning

Just A 'Flip' Of The Coin

Many games start with the flip of a coin. The Lord can flip things right side up faster than I can flip a coin. Things might look impossible to us when we're playing this game, but take heart. Watch how fast God flipped the coin of understanding for Cindy, Mike and Jessica. These three accounts look real good from His point of view. So let's take a moment and go up to the press box in this ballpark and view these three accounts from up there. In the ball park we get a better view from the press box. The Bibles declares the best view of this game is from the Holy of Holies. This fantastic view of things is given to all who have placed their trust in Jesus. Our present tense position is found in Eph 2:6 "and raised us up together, and made us 'sit' together in the heavenly places ..." (NKJV) From here we see things from God's point of view as we receive His perspective. Watch……..

God's first coin 'flip'

Cindy gained confidence in my wife as she heard me bragging about Bev to the audience of a seminar I was giving. Cindy asked if she could share something with Bev that had been bothering her for years. The woman told Bev

115

that she had stolen her Dad's prized and valuable coin collection when she was a young girl, and the guilt has been eating her up.

Bev asked her if she had asked God to forgive her. Cindy said she did, but the guilt remained. Bev showed Cindy from the Bible Acts 24:16 "This *being* so, I myself always strive to have a conscience without offense toward God and men." (NKJV)

Bev pointed out that Cindy could only have a clear conscience if she asked both God and her dad to forgive her. Cindy said, "Telling Dad would be the hardest thing in the world for me to do. Every time I think of doing that, I panic inside. I don't think I can."

Bev said, "Don't do this for your dad, or for yourself, do this for Jesus. You went against Jesus when you took the coins. Obey Him now and He will set you free. He'll give you the grace you need to handle the consequences of how your dad might respond. Knowing how hard it is to ask forgiveness can help keep us from doing wrong the next time we're tempted. Bev encouraged her to tell her dad, even though she's married now with grown children of her own.

Several weeks later Cindy wrote Bev a letter saying that she did tell her Dad and asked him to forgive her. Cindy felt immediate relief from the guilt she carried all those years.

Her Dad totally surprised her when he said, "I often wondered who took the coins. I'm glad it was you. You have always been very special to me. I knew the person who took my coins would be miserable until they confessed. Yes, I forgive you. I'm sure you have already suffered more than any discipline I would have given. I'm glad you told me. Don't you feel better now?"

The letter continued, "Thanks Bev for encouraging me to do the right thing. God gave me a very special father on earth and God is a wonderful Father in heaven! Thanks again!!"

God's second coin 'flip'

At one of my seminars a mother named Kathy stated that her son Mike was in a ministry on the East Coast. Mike let his hair grow long so he would look like the guys he was trying to reach for the Lord. The long hair didn't bother his parents; it was his Grandfather who was upset about it.

Mike had returned for a visit, and met his parents at the seminar before they returned together to their hometown. Kathy wanted me to speak with him, and tell him to cut his hair. Kathy told me that Mike's grandfather said he didn't want Mike coming to his house looking like a woman. The grandfather was not a Christian. He didn't understand the young man's heart or his ministry.

At his mother's request, Mike came up to me during a break between the sessions. He had a bandana around his head to hold most of his hair in place. Mike said. "My mom told me you think I should cut my hair.

I laughed and said, "No! I told your Mom, I would talk to you about your hair if you wanted me to. I think your Mom feels strongly about this for the sake of your grandfather. Your mom attended a session I gave where I declared that children should obey their parents."

Mike wanted to serve the Lord in the way he felt led. I asked him how long he had been involved in this ministry, and he replied, "About two years."

I asked, "How did your Grandfather know you had long hair?"

He said, "I send pictures and write letters to Mom and Dad from time to time so they know how my ministry is going."

I told Mike that his hairstyle is to be regulated by parents when the teenager is under the authority of the parents while living in their home. At the same time the teenager's hairstyle is not to be regulated by a minister, youth pastor, or a seminar leader like me.

I said, "You are out from under your parent's roof and therefore, out from under their direct authority. Being an adult, out on your own, you are under God's authority through your ministry. You can listen to your parent's counsel and use it or reject it. They will always have your best interest in mind, so it's always good to consider what they say. I'm sure your mom's comment to cut your hair came as a surprise to you since both your parents support your ministry."

He agreed that it was a surprise because his parents knew why he looked this way. Their concern was based on how Grandpa felt.

I said, "Since we're brothers in Christ, I thought it would be a good idea to look at this situation from God's point of view, which is called, 'wisdom'. He agreed, so I asked Mike some questions.

I asked him if he knew any of these guys he saw on the beaches before walking up to them.

He said, "No, I didn't know any of them."

I continued, "You told me the love you have for the Lord prompted you to walk up to complete strangers to share the Gospel with them and that's great. Your fear of them rejecting you and your message didn't keep you from your goal to reach out to them did it?"

He said, "No. I love the Lord, and I will do anything He tells me to do that will further His Kingdom.

I said, "Mike, we have a kindred spirit, and I appreciate your great attitude. Let me ask you a silly question. How long have you known your grandfather?"

He laughed and said, "All the years I can remember."

I said, "Do you love him?"

He said, "Of course I do!"

I asked, "Do you want to reach those guys on the beaches, whom you don't know, more than you want to reach your own Grandpa, whom you love and have known all your life?"

He said, "No, of course not."

I said, "Do you love him enough to cut your hair?"

He said, "Wait a minute! Short hair will hinder my ministry when I go back to the beaches."

I laughed and said, "Hey Sampson, your hair will grow back. If any of those guys on the beaches ask you why you cut your hair you can say, 'Because, I love my grandpa.' This will give them a real picture of what Christianity is all about."

Two weeks later I received an envelope full of Mike's hair. He did cut his hair and his grandpa asked Jesus Christ to come into his heart. Wow! He did reach his grandpa. Is God good or what? He sure flipped that coin. God really blessed Mike as he obeyed the call to show deference to his grandpa. Then grandpa, being honored, allowed Mike to share his faith, and with wonderful results. It also gave a wonderful addition to the story Mike will be able to tell those guys on the beaches while his hair grows back. Sampson came alive.

Is there anything the Lord would have you give up so He can use your sacrifice to reach someone else for whom Jesus died? This story encouraged me to let go when God says to let it go, regardless of what it might be. Go ahead and put it in an envelope, if you can, and send it to me.

My address is Jon Burnham - % Family Focus USA - P O Box 1 - Peoria, IL 61650.

You would be surprised at what I receive in the mail.

God's third coin 'flip'

Have you ever had an argument with someone you felt like you couldn't lose because you had support that could not be denied? If someone still denies what you know is true, what do you do? It happened to Jessica. She had reverted to childlike behavior to win the argument, and it didn't work. She finally won, but how did she do it? God flipped this coin, and again, it landed right side up.

Jessica called me from Nebraska after attending our seminar.

She said, "Don't I have a right to win an argument?

I said, "No."

Jessica said, "Jon, I was quoting the definition of a word, and my husband said, 'that is not the correct definition of that word.'

I said, "Yes it is, and I will prove it to you. I opened Webster's Dictionary and read the definition of the word to my husband. I was exactly right as per Webster. Do you know what my husband said? 'What does Webster know?' Jon, tell me. Don't I have a right to win an argument with Webster backing me up?"

Let me pause here before going on and explain, from scripture, why I said, "No".

I'll take you back to what I shared during the seminar that she attended.

Gen 22:1-2 and 7- 12 1-2 "Later on, God tested Abraham's faith and obedience. "Abraham!" God called. "Yes, Lord?" he replied. "Take with you your only son—yes, Isaac whom you love so much—and go to the land of Moriah and sacrifice him there as a burnt offering upon one of the mountains which I'll point out to you!". ....".

7-12 "Father," Isaac asked, "we have the wood and the flint to make the fire, but where is the lamb for the sacrifice?" "God will see to it, my son," Abraham replied. And they went on. When they arrived at the place where God had told Abraham to go, he built an altar and placed the wood in order, ready for the fire, and then tied Isaac and laid him on the altar over the wood. And Abraham took the knife and lifted it up to plunge it into his son, to slay him. At that moment the Angel of God shouted to him from heaven, "Abraham! Abraham!" "Yes, Lord!" he answered. "Lay down the knife; don't hurt the lad in any way," the Angel said, "for I know that God is first in your life—you have not withheld even your beloved son from me." (TLB)

When Sarah was ninety years old she became pregnant with Isaac. Later it says in Gen. 22 "God called Abraham to give his only son, yes, Isaac back to God." As we read the story we see that God tested Abraham's faith to see if he would give God his most prized position, Isaac. Abraham did, and he trusted God to bring Isaac back to life. Man, what faith!

How does this play out in Jessica's life winning an argument about a word definition? She said, "Don't I have a right to win an argument with Webster backing me up?" I said, "No."

When we give our lives to the Lord, we are really giving Him everything we have. The time we find ourselves arguing is a wake up call. The proof that we did not yield all we have to God is proven when we get angry about our rights and expectations being violated. If we don't have rights and expectations, because we gave them all to God, there is nothing to be upset about. If we have given everything to God, we will experience peace of mind, and there will be no need to argue over who won or who is winning an argument.

You may say, "Wait just a minute. God gave Isaac back to Abraham." Yes, He did, but not as Abraham's son. When God gave Isaac back to Abraham, he viewed Isaac as His property. We will tend to treat God's property better than we will treat our own property. When we give our mate, our children etc. to God, we will realize that we answer to God as to how we treat His property.

I asked Jessica why she was upset. She said, "If I don't win this argument he will think he won. He's wrong, and I have to show him, he's wrong. If I don't point this out to him, I'm not being a very good wife. I'm supposed to be his help meet."

I gave her this illustration. "There was a little five year old neighbor boy who was coming home from school with his mom. Nearing his home he asked his mom if he could tell Mrs. Jones what he learned in school today. The mother said, "Sure, Bobby. Then come right home."

Bobby ran up on Mrs. Jones's porch and knocked on the door. Mrs. Jones came to the door and Bobby said with great excitement, "Mrs. Jones's. Do you know what I learned in school today?" Mrs. Jones said, "What did you learn?" Bobby said, "I learned that two plus two is five." Mrs. Jones smiled and said, "No Bobby, two plus two is four." Bobby said, "It's five, it's five, it's five!"

Now, do you think Mrs. Jones said, "No!!! A thousand times no!!! I said it's four, and I'm older and smarter than you. You go home and tell your Mom, she should wash your mouth out with soap. Now get off my porch!!!" No, she wouldn't say that. Most likely Mrs. Jones would say, "Ok Bobby." Please come back tomorrow, and tell me what else you learned." I asked Jessica, "Why would she be so calm? Bobby doesn't belong to her, and Bobby is only five years old."

I continued, "You have a husband that came up with a childish five year old statement, 'What does Webster know?' Just as Mrs. Jones wouldn't argue with a five-year-old boy who doesn't belong to her, you would not argue with a husband who holds on to a childish five-year-old position and doesn't belong to you. Give your husband to God. Then treat him that way. Trust God to teach him."

Jessica called me a few weeks later. "Jon, you will never believe what happened. I gave my husband to God as the Bible suggested. My husband came into the kitchen, where I was washing dishes, and made a childish five-year-old comment. I didn't whirl around and argue like I used to. I simply said, "Really? I see." He left the kitchen for a few minutes but came back in, and repeated what he said before. I said, "That's nice dear." He left the kitchen, came right back in and said, 'You're no fun. Why won't you argue with me?' I said, "I don't want to argue with the man I love." He hugged me, and we talked about my giving him to the Lord, so I would treat him better, and he said, 'I want what you have.' Jon, my husband asked Jesus into his heart right there in the kitchen. I gave my husband to God, and He gave my husband back as a Christian man. I won't have any trouble giving everything else I own to God." God showed another quick 'flip' when the coin is in His hand.

Have you given your whole coin collection to God? They are more valuable in His hand. He wants us to trust Him with all we have, so we can have peace of mind. He gives us the power to be responsible with those coins because he owns them. We will treat His coins better than we treated our own coin collection.

God flipped the neighbor's car coin

I was standing in the front yard with Bev when our next-door neighbor drove by, and we noticed the front of his car was smashed. By the looks of the car, I was amazed that he could still drive it. He looked fine but the car was nearly totaled. Why was I not all upset? It wasn't my car. I had compassion for the neighbor, but it was not my car.

God flipped my car coin

Shortly after that I drove home from work and noticed our family car had a deep crease in the passenger side from the front to the back. I asked Bev what happened, and she told me that she had headed into a parallel parking place instead of backing into the spot. She scrapped the passenger side on the bumper of a parked truck. The scrap didn't hurt the truck at all but simply added a coat of our car's paint to the edge of the truck's front bumper.

Bev was waiting for me to blow sky high, but I didn't. She said, "Why aren't you upset?" I said, with a smile on my face, "It's not my car." We both laughed. I had given the car to God, and if He wants to check me out, to see if I really did give it to Him, that's His business. I'm responsible to fix it, change the oil and take care of 'His car'. Having given everything to God proves to be an on going blessing.

Since God can flip my car coin, He can sure flip Lee's bike coin

Lee worked hard earning money by mowing lawns and doing whatever so that he could buy a special bike. One day he finally had enough to buy the bike.

It wasn't long after that when I noticed he failed to put his bike in the garage. He wasn't taking care of his brand new bike; after all he said it was his bike.

One day I drove into the driveway, and I noticed Lee was popping wheelies on his new bike. He would get up some speed in the street and head toward the curb. At the last minute Lee would pull back on the handlebars and jerk the front wheel up to just miss the curb. One time he didn't calculate his 'jerk ' and bent the wheel as he hit the curb. Now the bike could not be ridden unless, of course, Lee wanted to jar his body from head to toe with each rotation of the front tire.

I saw this whole thing, and Lee saw me looking at him with a smile on my face. He said, "No big deal Dad; it's my bike. I bought it with my own money."

I smiled and asked Lee if he knew who owned the car that was parked in the drive way. I had just driven home so it seemed a silly question.

Lee said, "It's your car, Dad."

I said, "Lee, who owns the car parked in the drive way?"

A light went on in Lee's face, and he said, "Oh that's right, you gave everything to God; that's God's car."

I said, "Right." I just looked at Lee and then at his bike, smiled and started walking toward the house.

Lee said, "Come on, Dad, what are you smiling about?"

I said, "Lee, I'm just watching how you ride your bike. One day you will want to drive God's car. I'm responsible for the care of God's car. As I watch how you ride your bike, I'm thinking ahead as to how you might drive God's car, that's all." I smiled and walked into the house.

I noticed that Lee went to the store and purchased a new front wheel. He started putting the bike in the garage at night; he polished the bike, and kept it cleaned up etc. I was glad to see that because Bev and I had a goal to throw the keys to the car to Lee, without fear, on his sixteenth birthday.

When Lee turned sixteen Bev and I had the thrill of throwing Lee the keys to her car. He thanked us, took the keys and asked if he could drive the car around the block before supper. We said, "Sure." We haven't seen Lee since then. Maybe you have seen him? He's about five feet ten and weighs about 170 lbs......... "Just kidding."

God can flip any kind of coin

I was watching Mark play baseball when Jake came up and said, "Jon, I had an experience with Darrin, a former friend of mine who is also a farmer. I was just wondering what you would do in a situation like this. You counsel people all the time so maybe you can help me."

I said, "I would be glad to try. What happened?"

He said, "When you hear the story you'll be as upset as I am right now."

I asked, "What did Darrin do?"

He said, "Darrin noticed that I had finished spreading manure, and was ready to store the manure spreader until I needed it again. He asked if he could borrow it, and I said, 'Sure'. Months went by, and he didn't bring my manure spreader back. One day I was driving by Darrin's place in my truck and decided to stop and see what happened. No one was home, but I noticed that my manure spreader was behind his barn, so I drove up, hooked it up and began to drive away when I notice that the back axle was broken. I had to go home and bring my wagon back to haul the spreader home. I was ticked to say the least. It cost me an arm and a leg to fix it."

"I know Darrin pretty well. When he notices that my manure spreader is gone, from behind his barn, he'll figure I came over and took it. He is so bold that when he sees that it's fixed, he'll ask to use it again. I don't want to loan it to him again". Then he said, "What would you do?"

I asked him if he had ever thought to give God the manure spreader. He said, "What would God want with my manure spreader?" I said, "God can take care of what He owns better than you can." He asked, "How do I give God my manure spreader?" I said, "The same way you gave Him your life. He'll take whatever you give Him and then watch what He can do with it." My friend said, OK, I'll do that, but what do I tell this guy when he wants to use it again?" I said, "Tell him you gave it away. When he asks, 'Who did you give it to?' Tell him you gave it to God. Call me and tell me what he says."

Two weeks later Darrin called me and said, "You won't believe what happened. That farmer I was telling you about came over, noticed I had fixed the spreader and asked if he could use it again.

I said, 'I'm sorry, I can't loan it to you.'

He asked, 'Why not?'

I told him I gave it away.

He said, 'Well who did you give it to, I'll borrow it from him.'

I said, 'I gave it to God.'

"Jon, you should have seen the look on his face. He looked at me and said, 'never mind.' He walked away, climbed back in his truck and left. I don't have to worry about anything of mine again because God showed me, right then and there, how He handles what He owns. I saw Him put the fear of God in that man. When I saw Darrin's reaction, I gave everything I have to God. Thanks, Burnham."

I said, "God alone can put the fear of God in a man's mind when a man is thinking of using what belongs to God." As you read these stories are you more inclined to give the Lord all you own, all you think you have a right to and all your expectations? If you have already trusted Jesus with your life, giving him everything else is a lot easier.

I have laid out my coin collection to encourage you to give up your collection to God. You'll be glad you did.

15ᵗʰ Inning

Quit In The 'Middle' Of An Inning?

Ihave had times of frustration when trying to understand how to help people. I found out that God gave me certain responsibilities along with His grace to handle them. I found that I don't get frustrated when I play the game in the position the 'Coach' gave me. If you are frustrated see what the Coach told a minister named, Ted. He not only finished the inning, he played the rest of the game.

Ted, a minister, was really downcast when he called. He was frustrated and wanted to leave the ministry. He lived seventy miles away and didn't feel free to talk about his frustration with anyone close to home. He wanted to talk with someone who would use scripture to confirm that he was right in wanting to get out of the ministry.

Ted said he had listened to our radio program for years and knew that we use only the Word of God when counseling. I opened in prayer, and he followed with a heart felt prayer indicating that he truly wanted God's will in this decision.

Ted said, "I work all week long preparing my sermon because I want the people to understand what God is saying to them. I completed what I thought was a good message for this past Sunday's Sermon. I said all I could to make my three points and a poem clear to the congregation, so they would go home feeling fed by their shepherd. On Monday morning, my day off, Sid, a man in our congregation, came over to our home. Sid asked me a question that was answered in every way possible in my sermon. Jon, I quit! I'm getting out of the ministry. What a waste of time to prepare all week long, and then have Sid come to my home, on my day off, and tell me that he didn't understand the points I had worked so hard to make absolutely clear."

I said, "That's too bad."

Ted said, "What's too bad?"

I said, "That you think it's your job that he understands you."

Ted said, "Then why am I preparing a sermon all week if someone doesn't understand?"

I said, "It isn't your job to make him understand. That's God's job. Your job is to prepare the sermon, and it's God's job to help the man understand. No wonder you are ready to quit. God never intended for you to make anyone understand. You are in God's territory when you try to do what only God can do.

He said, "Where do you find that in Scripture?"

I asked him to turn to Psalms 37:1-11 TLB

I asked him to take a sheet of paper and draw a line down the middle of it. On the right hand side he was to title that column, "God's Job." On the left hand side, he was to title that left hand column - 'My Job'.

I asked him to read the first verse and tell me which side it should be on. We went through every verse, and it looked like this.

| My Job | God's Job |

Ps 37:1-11

1. Never envy the wicked!

2. Soon they fade away like grass and disappear.

3. Trust in the Lord instead. Be kind and good to others;

then you will live safely here in the land and prosper, feeding in safety.

4. Be delighted with the Lord.

Then he will give you all your heart's desires.

5. Commit everything you do to the Lord. Trust him to help you do it,

and he will.

6. Your innocence will be clear to everyone. He will vindicate you with the blazing light of justice shining down as from the noonday sun.

7. Rest in the Lord; wait patiently for him to act. Don't be envious of evil men who prosper.

8. Stop your anger!
   Turn off your wrath.
   Don't fret and worry—
   it only leads to harm.

9. For the wicked shall
   be destroyed,

but those who trust the Lord   shall be given every
                               blessing.

10. Only a little while
   and the wicked shall
   disappear.

You will look for them in
vain.

11. But all who humble themselves before the Lord

                               shall be given every
                               blessing and shall
                               have wonderful
                               peace. TLB

Ted jumped to his feet and clicked his heels. "That's it! He said, I have been thinking it's my job to get the people to understand. If they did understand I might take some credit for it, since I was the one who prepared the sermon all week. Thank you Jon, I'm going home to the congregation the Lord entrusted to me." He went to the outer office, grabbed his wife, hugged her and said, "I'm staying in the ministry!"

Now ask yourself, "What am I doing that frustrates me?" If you are frustrated it is a good indication that you are in the Lord's territory trying to do what only He can do. He never gives us grace to do His job. He gives us all the grace we need to do what's on our side of the ledger in Ps 37. Stay on your side or you will suffer the natural consequences of frustration and possibly, burnout.

16th Inning

Have You Ever Been Benched?

Have you ever been a way from home and received a devastating phone call about the death of a loved one, or someone very close? Sally, a baby Christian and a sophomore in college received such a call from her mom. Sally was upset with the Coach and His game plan. She didn't know the Coach all that well so she came to some wrong conclusions. He had to bench her for just a short time, so she would play her position in a way that would help the whole team, and not allow the enemy to score. Her response to Him was a blessing for the rest of the team to see and the enemy was held scoreless that inning.

Bev and I were sitting at home one afternoon when the phone rang. It was Charlie. He attended the high school meetings we held in our home every week.

Charlie said, "Jon, I met Sally here at college; she asked Christ into her heart last year as a freshman. Two months into this year, I heard her yelling at a classmate, 'There is no God. I'm an atheist.' Sally went on and on like that until I reminded her what I knew about her conversion to Christ last year. She said, 'Something happened at home yesterday that made me not want to trust God, if there is God! I don't want to talk about it. I just want to go home.' "

Charlie said, "Jon, Sally is determined to quit college and go home. She asked if I would drive her to Saint Louis, Missouri, where she lives with her parents. I told her that I would drive her home on one condition. On the way, we could stop in Morton, Illinois to speak with you and Bev about what happened. Sally said she would do that if it was the only way she could get a ride home. Jon, will you and Bev talk to her if I can get her there?"

I said. "Sure Charlie. Thanks for asking"

We set the approximate time to meet. Bev and I prayed that what we said to Sally would be used of God to help her and bring glory to Him.

It wasn't long until Charlie was at our door with Sally. He said, "Hi Jon. I would like to introduce you to my friend, Sally. I'll be back in one hour."

The look on Sally's face screamed that she didn't want to be here. I asked, "Would you like to come in?" She said, "Well, I'm here, so I might as well if I want a ride the rest of the way home."

Sally came in and sat on the davenport across from Bev and me in the living room. I asked her to explain what had happened two months into her sophomore year.

She said, "First off, don't you think for a minute that what you say will change my mind to go home!"

I assured her that this was not our intent.

She went on to say, "I became a Christian last year at college. After my freshman year, I went back home, and I told my friend Jerry what happened to me, and I began to witness to him. Jerry was a guy I had known since grade school. He was not really my boyfriend; he was just a good friend. I told Jerry that I was going to heaven, but he wasn't interested. I witnessed to him all summer. Jerry wasn't fighting me; but he did not make a decision. I went back to college in the fall and was only there two months when I received a phone call from Mom telling me that Jerry was riding his motorcycle over some railroad tracks, and a train hit him. They took Jerry to the hospital where they pronounced him dead. That's not fair. How could a loving God let that happen? No. I don't think there is a God. If there is a God, I don't want anything to do with Him if He would allow something like that to happen."

I asked Sally if I could tell her a story that might help.

She said, "Yes, but remember what I said, ' Nothing you say will change my mind. I'm going home!"

I nodded and continued, "Bill was a Christian sailor hitchhiking from Chicago, Illinois heading for St. Louis, Missouri. As he was waiting, he prayed for someone to pick him up with whom he might be able to witness about his faith in Jesus Christ. A short time later Mr. Clark, a distinguished looking businessman in his mid seventies, pulled over and asked Bill where he was headed. Bill told him, and Mr. Clark offered him a ride. About twenty minutes into the ride, the conversation changed from a secular one to a spiritual one. Bill felt free to share how he had become a Christian. In his mind he was thanking God for answering his prayer. All of a sudden, Mr. Clark pulled the car over to the side of the road. Bill thought he had gone too far sharing his faith. Mr. Clark turned off the motor, looked at Bill and said, "Do you think it's too late for an old man like me to get what you have?"

Bill was thrilled with the question, and said, "No sir! You can ask Jesus into your heart right here and now."

This is what Mr. Clark said as he followed Bill in prayer. "Dear Jesus. I've done a lot of things wrong over these many years. I agree that those things were sins. Thank you for taking my place on the cross and shedding your blood to wash them away. I'm asking you to come into my heart to be my Savior and Lord. Please help me the rest of my life. Thank you for hearing and answering my prayer. I pray this in Jesus. Amen.

After Mr. Clark finished praying, he started the car, and they drove to St. Louis as brothers in Christ. When they arrived in St. Louis, Mr. Clark gave Bill his card and asked him to look him up if he was ever in New York City."

"Seven years later Bill had become a business man and happened to be in New York City. He had carried Mr. Clark's card all those years and was anticipating a great reunion with him. He arrived at the address on the card and knocked on the door. A woman, in her late seventies, answered the door, and said with a gruff voice, "What do you want?" Bill said, "Does Mr. Clark live here?" She said, "What do you want with him?" Bill said, "Well, seven years ago I was hitch-hiking from Chicago to St. Louis, Mr. Clark picked me up, and I shared my faith with him; he asked Jesus to be his Savior and Lord." Mrs. Clark burst into tears and asked Bill to come in. Bill asked if he had said something wrong. Mrs. Clark said, "No, but the very day he dropped you off in St. Louis, he was found dead of a heart attack in his hotel room."

She continued, "I'm crying because I've been shaking my fist at God for letting him die before he became a Christian. I had been praying for him for forty years, and I thought God didn't answer my prayers. Now here you are, telling me that you led my husband to Christ. I have wasted seven years of my life assuming that God let me down. I feel so foolish. I can't thank you enough for being faithful to share your faith with my husband and coming here to make contact with him, or I would have gone to my grave thinking God failed me."

I looked at Sally and asked, "How many years do you want to waste?"

She said, "What do you mean?"

I said, "How long were you in college before your friend died?"

She said, "Two months."

I asked, "You hadn't seen him for two months?"

She nodded. I asked, "How many moments did it take for you to ask Jesus into your heart?"

She said, "Just a few moments. Why?"

I asked, "How many moments are in two months?"

She said, "Thousands of moments."

I asked, "Is it possible that Jerry could have received Jesus Christ into his life in just a few of those moments, during the two months you hadn't seen him?"

She agreed. I asked her again, "How many years do you want to waste?"

She said, 'none!'

She followed me in prayer and rededicated her life to Christ. When Charlie returned to pick her up, she said, "Will you take me back to college?" Needless to say Charlie was thrilled, for he had been praying for her during that hour we talked.

I hope you haven't wasted any time because you thought the Lord didn't come through for you. Yes, His timing is perfect. When you get to heaven, He won't even have to tell you why things happened to you as they did, because you will have the mind of Christ, knowing the end from the beginning. Won't that be something?

17th Inning

This Inning Was Full of Bad Calls

Have you ever been wounded by someone close to you? Not wounded by a gun, but by finding out something that hurt so badly you felt as though someone was turning a knife in the pit of your stomach? We tend to hold a grudge when that happens, and the first place it will show is on your face. When giving a speech in Iowa, I saw Angie in the audience. According to what I saw on her face, she may have had a history of sharp pains in her stomach.

At break time Angie came up and said, "I like what I heard Monday and Tuesday, but tonight you are going to talk about forgiveness. If you see me frowning in the audience, don't take it personally. I have a great deal of bitterness toward my parents. I've gone to one minister after another, and none of them has been able to help me. Since you are not a minister, I really don't have any confidence that you can help me either." I told Angie that I was not offended because I have never helped anyone get rid of bitterness, but I know of someone who can. I didn't tell Angie that I noticed the painful look on her face the very first session.

I asked her what caused her bitterness toward her parents. Angie said, "When I was in the seventh grade, I was sitting in school one morning when the teacher started talking about some personal things that began to make me wonder about something. What the teacher said brought a thought forward that had been in the back of my mind for a several months, so I decided to check it out. I jumped up out of my chair, left the classroom, and ran all the way home. I ran into the house, and opened a metal box where my parents keep their important papers. I was looking for their marriage certificate. Dad and Mom never talked with me about their lives before they were married. I thought it a bit strange that they celebrated their wedding anniversary in private. I wondered if I was conceived before they were married. When I saw the date on the marriage certificate I was devastated. I was inside my mom six months before they married. It burns me to think about it. There is a name in the Bible for someone like me. I will have to carry that name with me the rest of my life. I wanted to run away right then, but I didn't. I wanted to see the look on their faces when I showed them their marriage certificate, and my birth certificate."

She said, "All this sounds pretty awful doesn't it?"

I said, "What happened when your parents arrived home?"

Angie continued, "They came in the door together, and I held up the two certificates, but didn't say a word. Dad did. What he said made me feel like a knife was twisting in my stomach.

He said, "You ingrate! How dare you confront us! We took care of you all these years. We fed you, bathed you, clothed you, and took care of you when you were sick. Who do you think you are? Are you going to judge us for that moment of passion? God could have stopped that pregnancy, but He didn't."

She went on to say, "What really hurt was the fact that Mom never said a word. She just looked down and let Dad yell at me. By the way, Jon, My parents are both active in the church. They teach Sunday school and are well thought of in the community. I couldn't wait to get out of that house, so I took the first opportunity I had and married right out of high school at the age of seventeen. Another thing, I didn't go to their thirtieth wedding anniversary. Can you see why no one has been able to help me get rid of this bitterness?"

I asked, "If you had your first child out of wedlock, would you be less inclined to nail your parents?" Angie said, "I have to hand it to you Jon, that's where all the ministers started. They asked the same question, so I'll have to give you some credit since you're only a layman. My husband and I agreed not to even try to have children for the first year of our marriage so, if we had a premature baby, no one would think twice about it. No, we did everything we could so our first child would not have to go through what I did."

I asked Angie if any of the ministers talked about the balloon verse in scripture.

She said, "No, they didn't. What do you mean, balloon verse?"

I asked if Angie had ever done anything wrong.

She said, "Of course I have. Everyone has. I cheated in school and got in big trouble for it. I stole a package of gum at the drug store on the way home from school one day when I was in the sixth grade."

I asked if there was anything else.

She smiled and said, "Just the other day I asked my husband if I could have three dresses that were on sale, and he said I could have one. What my husband didn't know was that I wanted only one. If I had asked for only one, I'd have gotten none. I guess that was a lie, wasn't it?

"I said, "Let's take inventory. You cheated, you stole, and you lied."

She said, "Yes, but look what my parents did. Tell me, what is the balloon verse?"

I asked Angie to blow up an imaginary balloon. I said, "We're going to label that balloon 'Total Law'. I listed words such as murder, rape, fornication (sex before marriage), adultery, lying, cheating and stealing. Now that the balloon is blown up and has all these sins on it, I would like for you to take an imaginary pin, and stick it in your parent's word, 'Fornication'. That is how you came into the world. What happens to the balloon?"

She said, "It bursts."

I asked her to blow up another imaginary balloon, and she did. I asked her to stick a pin in one of her words, and she said, "Well, I just lied to my husband. I'll stick it in that word.

I asked her, "What happened to the balloon?"

Angie said, "It bursts! What about all these balloons?"

I told Angie that she had demonstrated the balloon verse in scripture.

She asked, "What is the balloon verse in scripture that you keep talking about?"

I handed her my Bible and pointed to the verse and asked her to read it out loud. This is what Angie read in James 2:10 "And the person who keeps every law of God but makes one little slip is just as guilty as the person who has broken every law there is." TLB

I asked Angie to tell me what it meant to her, and she said she wasn't sure. I told Angie that when I broke any one of those laws I was guilty of breaking every law there is.

I said, "What that means is this; I'm guilty of what your parents did."

Angie looked at me in horror, and said, "You did that too?"

I said, "No." Angie said, "Didn't you just lie to me?"

I said, "In God's sight, I didn't have to do what your parents did to be guilty of what your parents did. In fact, since you broke the law in one point, you are guilty of what your parents did."

I continued, "I want to paint a picture for you of what I think happened. You set up a little box at the foot of the cross. You stood on it, and looked down at your parents, because you didn't sin their sin. This verse removes that little box, so now you are on level ground with your parents and me. The ground at the foot of the cross is very flat. The verse means that we all need Jesus in our heart so that no one is elevated to look down on anyone else. Jesus is the only one elevated. Now we can look up with our praise and adoration, because He is no longer on the cross. What He did on the cross washed away everyone's sins, including your sins, my sins, and yes, even the sins of your Mom and Dad."

Angie became very sober and asked what she could do to correct what she had done?

I said, "I would go back home and tell your parents that you have not been treating them in a Christ-like manner. I would tell them that you have been wrong, and ask them to forgive you."

"Don't expect them to ask your forgiveness for what they did. If they do ask your forgiveness, you have a bonus on your hands. Yield the right that they will ever take care of what they did. You are only responsible to be like Christ. The Lord is the only One who can empower you to do that. Your joy will come in being obedient. You have allowed them to control your emotions long enough."

Are you letting anyone other than your Lord Jesus control your emotions? Remember the definition of bitterness? If it's painful to your mind to think of 'that' other person, you are bitter. It's like feeding yourself poison and expecting that other person to die. I wouldn't poison myself, so why would I let a person, for whom I have little affection, 'poison' me?

18th Inning

Wow! Two 'Big Mounds'

Good used His Word, and some of the smallest of His creation to free Zack from his unbiblical belief system. Zack chose the truth over what he had been taught by those who loved him. It came down to this statement. 'If what you believe isn't true, would you want to know it? Everyone should make sure that what he or she believes is true. Jesus said in John 8:32 "And you will know the truth, and the truth will set you free." (TLB) We cannot have an abundant life apart from the truth.

Mark was talking to Zack on a college campus. It wasn't very long before Mark was using the Bible to share his faith. Zack's belief system was different than what he was hearing from Mark. When Mark quoted what Jesus said in John 14:6 ...... "I am the way, the truth, and the life. No one comes to the Father except through Me." (NKJV) Zack was upset; he told Mark that Jesus was not the only way to God. Zack said, "God is in every living thing." In a huff, Zack walked away from Mark, left the campus, and headed for a local country road to walk off his anger.

As he walked down the road he looked over the fence and noticed a farmer, heading his way, plowing his field. Just thirty yards out in the field Zack noticed a mound of ants in the path of the tractor. Instinctively Zack jumped over the fence and headed toward the mound of ants. When he reached the mound he started to yell at the ants, "Get out of the way; you're going to get squashed."

In Zack's belief system God was in every one of those ants. The farmer drove his tractor right up to the mound of ants, turned off his tractor and watched.

Suddenly Zack stopped yelling at the ants and dropped to his knees in prayer. After praying Zack stood up, looked at the farmer and said, "I suppose you are wondering what I'm doing here."

The farmer nodded, and said, "I am a bit curious. Why were you yelling at those ants?"

Zack said, "I was taught that God is in every living thing. If you had kept plowing you would have killed a lot of these ants. I was yelling at them to get out of the way. Guess what? They didn't pay any attention to me."

The farmer asked, "Are you a college student?"

Zack said, "Yes."

The farmer replied, "I'm just a farmer, but I could have told you that."

Zack said, "You don't understand. If I could have become an ant I could have tweaked my antennae to warn the ants that they were going to get squashed. They would have understood me. But I couldn't become an ant. You know what? Some guy on campus told me that God became a man to tell me that I was headed for hell if I didn't check out this man named Jesus."

Farmer, I just asked Jesus to come into my heart. I'm going back to campus to find that guy, and tell him how God used him and this mound of ants, to get me to see that I needed Jesus as my Savior. Hey, farmer, I'm going to heaven when I die. Isn't that great?"

In this story I see two mounds from which God pitched to get through to Zack. Mark, the man on campus was the first mound God used to pitch His message to Zack. Then God used some of His smallest creatures to build a mound from which God would pitch His message again. Zack saw and heard His pitch twice. Zack heard the message that God loved him. Zack believed in Rom 10:17 "So then, faith comes by hearing, and hearing by the word of God."

When you hear God's word, He gives you enough faith to believe Him. Zack believed what he heard from God when He spoke from those two mounds.

Think back for a moment, and see how fortunate you are to have been given the truth. If you had loved ones who were sincere, but sincerely wrong, you can see how fortunate you are to have had God reveal His truth to you through His Word, and from a mound here or there. If you are one who is reading about the truth of God for the first time in this book, you can thank God that He 'delivered' the truth to you in this manner. God is faithful. If you have read this far, I can safely assume you have heard and seen His pitch. I pray that you have trusted Jesus like Zack did. You may want to run back and thank the one who told you about this book that is filled with His truth. You may want to become a mound from which God can pitch His truth.

19th Inning

He Saw The Signals From 'Home Plate'

Many people have a weakness in their private life, which they have justified in their own minds, even though they know it's wrong. If it ever became known, especially if they are Christians, they would be embarrassed and humiliated. The key question is, 'Do you want God or anyone else giving you instructions on what to do to have victory over that weakness?

Rex was in the batter's box and was trained to look for instructions from the third base Coach before every pitch. Rex was in the habit of ignoring the Coach's signals. The signal was to lay down a sacrifice bunt, but Rex wanted to hit the ball. Wanting to do his own thing was his weakness. Do you have a weakness like that? See what Rex did to have victory over this all to common weakness.

Rex was signaled to obey the Coach and make a sacrifice. Sacrifice what? Rex had developed the habit of drinking beer, an alcoholic beverage. The signal from God was to stop drinking beer. Instead, make a sacrifice. Lay it down.

Rex wanted his own way and justified drinking beer because it tasted good to him and didn't contain much alcohol. Rex would see a beer commercial on TV and couldn't keep from drooling until his thirst was satisfied. If you have a weakness like this, you will be amazed at what a picture will do to help you say "no" to yourself and "yes" to God. Take a look.

I suggested to Rex, "Picture this: Go up to the cross and tilt the Lord's head back so you can pour some liquor in His mouth. You will have to be the one to do it, because He can't use His hands, since they're nailed to the cross. While you're doing that, remember He is dying on the cross to wash away that very sin. Alcohol destroys brain cells; it can cause one to become drunk, and it can cause others to stumble. Isn't that a terrible mind picture?" He agreed.

I explained to Rex, "When you asked Jesus Christ to come into your heart, you immediately became part of Him, and you are now one with Him. Therefore, what are you doing when you drink liquor? Are you not putting the liquor into His mouth?" You may be thinking, "That's a stretch. Where is that in the Bible?"

We find in I Cor. 6:15 "Don't you realize that your bodies are actually parts and members of Christ?" (TLB)

I Cor. 6:19-20 "Haven't you yet learned that your body is the home of the Holy Spirit God gave you, and that he lives within you? Your own body does not belong to you. For God has bought you with a great price. So use every part of your body to give glory back to God because He owns it." TLB

Here the Bible tells us that when we put a bottle of liquor to our mouths, we are actually putting the bottle of liquor to the Lord's mouth, because our body is part of Christ's body. He tells us in these verses that our bodies do not belong to us. He owns them. He bought us with a great price when He died on the cross for us. God is giving us an opportunity to show we love Jesus and to bring Him glory. It says in I Cor 10:31 "Therefore, whether you eat or drink, or whatever you do, do all to the glory of God." (NKJV)

As Rex thought about this, he came to a sobering conclusion. "Wanting my own way caused me to ignore God's signal to sacrifice what tasted good to me; that could cause others to stumble, and tarnish God's reputation. I realized I could never drink beer to the glory of God. For me, it's a great way to show God, I love Him more."

Will you snap a picture that can help you conquer your weakness? God has given you the camera in your mind. Just aim and click. It will last a lifetime. Rex still drools when he sees a beer commercial, and he doesn't mind at all. It's an opportunity to love Jesus by accepting the signal to sacrifice.

The Second Signal:

David gives us an account of what happened to him in 2 Sam. 23:15-17 "David remarked, "How thirsty I am for some of that good water in the city well!" (The well was near the city gate.)

So the three men broke through the Philistine ranks and drew water from the well and brought it to David. However, he refused to drink it! Instead, he poured it out before the Lord. "No, my God," he exclaimed, "I cannot do it! This is the blood of these men who have risked their lives." TLB

Jesus did a whole lot more than risk His life; He gave His life and shed His blood to wash away our sins. How can this scriptural story about David give victory to a man who had a real problem drinking alcoholic beverages?

David refused to drink the water he craved for and there was nothing wrong with water. Instead, he poured it out before the Lord. Why? David said.........

"No, my God," he exclaimed, "I cannot do it! This is the blood of these men who have risked their lives."

David honored the men who risked their lives to get Him that water by pouring the water out on the ground even though there was <u>nothing wrong</u> with the water. Show God you honor what He did for you and pour the alcoholic beverage out on the ground. Besides, there are <u>several things wrong</u> with an alcoholic beverage.

These first two signals from Rex and David are very clear to help you make the right decision. This third signal comes from His creation to stimulate right thinking habits, not wrong drinking habits.

The Third Signal:

We have the privilege to refuse a drink that isn't good for us, a drink that doesn't bring glory to God and a drink that could cause someone to stumble. David refused to drink the water his men brought him because they had risked their lives to get it for him. We should refuse to drink liquor because Jesus sacrificed His life to set us free from liquor.

God's power can work on the weaknesses in a player's life. He gave us a brain to read His Word and to learn the right stance at home plate.

Consider! Who put the materials on the earth to make an alcoholic beverage in the first place? That's right. God did. However, He didn't make the liquor. Who made the mountain stream you see on beer commercials? God did, but He didn't intend for men to use the mountain stream for these commercials. Who gave men the high tech capability to create television so that we could see the beautiful mountain stream in the first place? God did. Even so, God didn't put that beer commercial on television. Did God create all these things just to entice people? Did He create all this just to tease people? Of course not!

The Bible says in James 1:13-15 "And remember, when someone wants to do wrong it is never God who is tempting him, for God never wants to do wrong and never tempts anyone else to do it. Temptation is the pull of man's own evil thoughts and wishes. These evil thoughts lead to evil actions and afterwards to the death penalty from God." (TLB)

God created our taste buds. Therefore, He knows how good alcohol can taste, especially when one has acquired a special taste for it. The Bible states in Col 1:16 "Christ himself is the Creator who made everything in heaven and earth, the things we can see and the things we can't; the spirit world with its kings and kingdoms, its rulers and authorities; all were made by Christ for his own use and glory." (TLB)

How can God use an alcoholic beverage for His own use and glory? Each time a person is tempted to drink something that will harm him, just to satisfy himself, he can choose not to drink and show that he loves Jesus more. I John 4:19 "We love him because he first loved us." (NKJV)

Jesus knows the sacrifice that person is making for Him by not drinking. He knows and appreciates that sacrifice because he empowered the sacrifice. It says in John 15:5... "for without Me you can do nothing." (NKJV)

A young couple, Sam and Penny, had visited a church several times, and they wanted to talk to the pastor about joining, even though they didn't think they qualified. He asked them what made them feel that way. Sam and Penny said, "We both drink alcoholic beverages, and we both smoke cigarettes. The pastor told them they could join his church if they had a personal relationship with Jesus Christ. He also told them they could bring a six-pack of beer and a pack of cigarettes, sit on the front row during a Sunday morning service, smoke, and drink while he preaches. He said, Sam and Penny, before you do that, please read this one verse of scripture found in I Cor. 10:31 "Therefore, whether you eat or drink, or whatever you do, do all to the glory of God." (NKJV)

Sam and Penny went home and didn't go back to the church that next Sunday, but they did return the following Sunday.

After the sermon they approached the pastor and said, "We would like to join your church."

The pastor looked pleased and asked them how they came to that decision.

They said, "After reading the scripture you gave us, we realized we couldn't drink, or smoke at home to the glory of God. If we couldn't drink and smoke to the glory of God at home, how could we possibly do that to the glory of God while sitting on the front row during a Sunday morning church service? We decided to quit drinking and smoking. Now we want to become members of this church. Jesus sacrificed His life for us, so we decided we could make a sacrifice and stop drinking and smoking for Him."

That was a very interesting sacrifice bunt they made at home plate. Are there things that you need to sacrifice to the Lord? You're at home plate and when He signals for you to bunt, go ahead and lay it down the first or third base line. You'll be glad you obeyed His signal to sacrifice. Not only could you move the runner to second base, you just might make it to first with the chance to be the winning run. There is much more ahead. The Bible states in I Cor. 2:9 "But as it are written: Eye has not seen, nor ear heard, nor have entered into the heart of man the things which God has prepared for those who love Him." (NKJV) We can't begin to know what the Lord wants to give us. Isn't this the greatest game in the world?

20th Inning

A 'Bonus' Inning

W hy did Phillip, a minister of a large church, hate me for over a year? He attended a seminar I was giving the year before and saw something he couldn't understand and it made him angry with me. However, he was blessed for his humility and obedience to do what God showed him to do. Notice that even a minister can get his Biblical priorities out of order. It's easier to get them out of order if you don't know what they are. Before reading any further, do you know what the five Biblical priorities are? Make a list of what you think they are, from the most important to the least. All are important, but when out of order, natural consequences follow. If you see, as Phillip did, that your list is out of order, what would you do? Let's see what Phillip did.

Phillip approached me during one of the breaks when I was giving a series of messages in Ohio. He said, "I've hated you for a whole year now. I came to your seminar last year in these same conference grounds. Within a matter of minutes, you had the audience eating out of your hand. I was jealous then, and I'm jealous now because you have affected this audience in the same way you did last year. I look at my congregation when I'm preaching, and the people are looking around showing little interest in what I'm saying. I know this isn't the proper way to approach you, but you often talk about hearing the still small voice of the Holy Spirit. I may not be sounding like a very spiritual minister right now, but I just had to tell you what the Holy Spirit told me as I was listening to you this morning. The Holy Spirit said, 'If you will humble yourself, and tell Jon how you have been feeling about him for the past year, I will tell you through Jon, why you have lost the attention of your congregation.' " Jon, I want to know. I have confidence that He will tell you what my problem is. Can I meet with you in the hotel lobby at nine o'clock tomorrow morning?"

I told Phillip I would be honored to meet with him. Bev and I went up to our hotel room, and I told her what the pastor said. I explained to Bev that I didn't have a clue what the pastor was talking about. He seemed to be a bold, honest man. Bev said, "Jon, I've heard you tell others that the Bible says in Matthew 10:19 "But when they deliver you up, do not worry about how, or what you should speak. For it will be given to you in that hour what you should speak;" (NKJV)

Bev and I dropped to our knees and asked the Lord to give me, within that hour, what the minister needed in his life. We knew the Lord would honor Phillip's obedience in humbling himself. It was exciting to visit Matt. 10:19 in real life, waiting for that hour to know what to say. This could turn out to be a bonus in disguise. How the Holy Spirit would get that through to me would be an exciting bonus.

The next morning I met Phillip in the lobby of the hotel. I asked him, " Pastor, when did you begin to notice this gap between you and your congregation?"

He said, "Last year it came to a head. I have a son who has not been close to me in years. Several times this year, while I was in the pulpit preaching, my son jumped on his motorcycle and began popping wheelies around the church building. It was very distracting, but I wanted to show that I was faithful to my calling to preach the Gospel. I kept right on preaching. I was sure the congregation would see my dedication to them and this ministry. That's why it bothers me so much when they show so little interest in my sermons. I work all week preparing a message that will help them."

I asked if there was anything else.

Phillip said, "My wife and I don't see eye to eye on as much as I would like but that's the way it is with many of the couples I counsel. It's the normal husband and wife thing."

I asked Phillip if he knew, from scripture, what his priorities are.

He said. "Yes. God is first. Since He is first, my work for Him is second. My wife and family are a close third. My wife knew what she was getting into when she married me. She knew that I wanted to be a minister and how dedicated I would be since God called me to this work. We were doing fine except for these last few years."

I asked Phillip where he learned his list of priorities.

He said, "Common sense shows me what they are as I read the Bible."

I asked him if he knew that they are listed specifically in Ephesians 5:18 through Ephesians 6:10.

He hadn't noticed that there was a list.

I said, "This list may be what God wants you to see. I told Phillip that Bev and I prayed that God would show me, within the hour, the problem he was concerned about last night. I know for a fact that when my priorities are out of order, I suffer the natural consequences.

Let's take a look in Eph 5:18-6:11 "Don't drink too much wine, for many evils lie along that path; be filled instead with the Holy Spirit and controlled by Him." (NKJV)

I said, "So the first priority is God, just as you said Pastor.

The mate is second. "Here is where your priorities differ from these in scripture. You said God is first and your ministry is second. The Bible says the Lord is first and your wife is second.. and it shows up here, "submitting to one another in the fear of God." (NKJV)

"These next few verses show the wife her role, and then the following few verses show the husbands role. As each one performs his or her individual role, each will show if God is truly number one or not." Verse 22 says, "Wives, submit to your own husbands, as to the Lord." (NKJV) If she is not submitting to her husband, it is a show and tell that she is not submitting to the Lord. "Then in verse 25 -29 God tells the husband how to treat the wife. " Husbands, love your wives, just as Christ also loved the church and gave Himself for her, (NKJV) It is not hard for a wife to submit to a husband when he is treating her in a Christ-like manner.

"Chapter 6 talks about your children being in the third position on the priority list. God doesn't mention the children until God has Dad and Mom viewing Him as number one, and each other as number two.

Eph 6:1-11 "Children, obey your parents in the Lord, for this is right. *"Honor your father and mother,"* which is the first commandment with promise: *"that it may be well with you and you may live long on the earth."* (NKJV) He then goes on to tell the parents how to treat the children. Since God is first and the mate is second they are now ready to properly handle the children who are the third priority as He states in verse 4. "And you, fathers, do not provoke your children to wrath, but bring them up in the training and admonition of the Lord." (NKJV)

"The fourth priority is our vocation. Being a minister is your vocation as found in Eph. 6:5 & 9

"Bondservants, (employee) be obedient to those who are your masters according to the flesh, with fear and trembling, in sincerity of heart, as to Christ; And you, masters, (employer) do the same things to them, giving up threatening, knowing that your own Master also is in heaven, and there is no partiality with Him." (NKJV)

The fifth priority is in verse 10-11 "Finally, my brethren, be strong in the Lord and in the power of His might. Put on the whole armor of God that you may be able to stand against the wiles of the devil." (NKJV) "The fifth priority suggests that if we have the first priorities in their proper order, we will have a ministry that will be used of God at any time – day or night. The fifth priority is our personal ministry having victory in how we live. Other people will want to know how we can live like this. A personal ministry may develop. The fifth priority may tend to float up above the others if we are not careful."

Phillip jumped up from his chair, ecstatically. He said, "My priorities are wrong. God used the resistance of my family and congregation to get my attention. Consequently, what do I do now?"

I said, "I would encourage you to explain to your wife, your son, and the congregation what you did wrong. Ask their forgiveness. God gives power to the humble. It would be good to tell them, 'With God's help, I purpose to keep my Biblical priorities in order from now on.'

He thanked me and was out of the lobby in a shot. What a joy to see a pastor excited about learning a lesson from the Lord through scripture, yes, within that hour.

How did you do? Did you write down all five? Did you have the priorities in order? Good for you.

See the next account and how God helped Chris, another pastor.

"Anyone" Can Have A Priority Problem

I met Chris, a pastor in Colorado who told me how diligent he was in carrying out his duties for his congregation. Chris said he was available to them twenty-four hours a day. He said he and his wife hadn't taken a family vacation for the last seven straight years. I looked at his wife as she glanced up at me. What did I see on her face? You guessed it. Frustration. Her expression indicated her husband had removed her from the number two spot on God's priority list.

During the Biblical priority session of the seminar, I suggested to the congregation that they not take an offering for me that night. Instead, they could take an offering big enough for the pastor and his family to go on their first vacation in seven years. The wife looked at me from her seat in the audience and said, "Thank you". Guess what? I received another invitation to come back the following year to give another seminar. You know who was behind that invitation. I know that the godly list of scriptural priorities can keep a pastor from losing his marriage, family, congregation, and his ministry.

I hope and pray that as you read these stories you will continue to keep your priorities in Biblical order. If they are out of order the Lord will show you, through natural consequences, until He gets your attention, just like he got mine.

I had put my teen ministry above my wife and children. One evening at our home, when I was talking to several teenagers, a girl came up to me and said, 'Jon, do you love your kids?' I said, 'Sure I do. Why do you ask?' She said, 'Why don't you pay any attention to them?'

Bev, Lee, Mark and Holly benefited from the observation of that teenage girl. It hurt me at the moment, and it should have. No pain, no gain. Shortly after that I heard what the priorities should be. God, mate, children, job and if these are in order, God will give you a ministry with others, no matter if it's a one on one ministry, or one that puts you in front of a group of people. God will use you the way He intended. Whenever I begin to have troubles, I can usually trace it to my priorities slipping out of order. I have to take inventory often to keep this from happening. If you are reading this when the wife wants your attention, please put this book down.

21st Inning

Dad Hit Two Home Runs

Dad, if you have children who are not prone to give you the kind of attention you crave, and your heart is breaking, I'm sure you will be interested to see what Scott did about that problem and how his boys responded to him. If you are not directly affected by this story, you may know of someone who needs to read it. You might be used to help them score in the game they are playing.

Scott, a Christian dad, came to me with a sad story. He said that his seven-year-old and nine year old boys never called him Dad. They never said they loved him. Scott explained, "They'll come into the house, walk right by me, and neither one of them will acknowledge me. I bought them each a bike, and a baseball glove, and they never said thanks. They don't say, 'Hi' or anything. It's as though I'm not in the room. Where did this come from? I can't figure it out. This really hurts deep down inside, and I don't know what to do about it."

I asked Scott what kind of relationship he had with his Dad. He said that he was never close to his dad. He said, "Come to think of it, he never said he loved me, and I never said that to him. How can I change from being just like my Dad?"

I asked Scott what kind of relationship he had with God. He said he was a Christian. He asked Jesus into his heart four years ago. I said, "Do you talk to God the Father?" Scott said, "Not really. My own Dad didn't listen to me so why would God listen to me?" I said, "Why are you letting your own Dad paint a picture in your mind of what God the Father is like?" Could it be that almighty God is quite different from your Dad? It is all too common for a youngster to think that God must be like his Dad."

I asked Scott if he reads the Bible.

He said, "Yes, I read along with the pastor when he reads a few verses in his sermon."

I asked if that was the only time he reads, and he said yes.

I said, "Let's take inventory here. You want your boys to pay attention to you. Couldn't God the Father be using your boys to show you how He feels when you don't pay any attention to Him?" Scott agreed.

I asked, "Would you like to ask God to forgive you for not giving Him the attention He deserves; would you like to discover what He is really like?"

Scott asked his Father in heaven to forgive him, and asked the Lord to help him draw his boys to God and to himself. Scott ended up purposing to get into the Word of God for a minimum of five minutes every day.

I explained to Scott, "One can read a whole chapter of scripture in five minutes. You will begin to see that God the Father loves you as much as he loves His own Son as pointed out in John 17. When you begin to see the proper picture of what your Father in heaven is really like, then pass that picture on to your boys."

I said, "You can ask the Lord to give you the boldness you need to show your boys you love them. The Bible says, 'Love begets love.' Start out slowly. Go into their bedroom tonight, kneel by your oldest son's bed, and say something like this, 'Lord, thanks for Jimmy. Help me be the kind of Dad you want me to be. I pray this in Jesus name. Amen.'

"Then get up and go over to Billy's bed, kneel down and say the same thing. Don't expect either one of them to say anything in return. As you're leaving the room, say, 'Love you guys.' Do that every night, then come back and tell me what happened."

Two weeks later Scott came into my office all smiles. I said, "What happened?" He said, "I couldn't believe it. The first night was the hardest for me not knowing what they would do. I did and said just what you told me. Jimmy rolled over and hugged the other side of the bed and didn't say a word. It broke my heart, but I prayed what you told me anyway. Then I went to Billy's bed and knelt down and prayed in front of him. He just looked at me as if to say, 'What is this strange thing that's happening?'

"I jumped up and went to the door and as I left, I said, 'Love you guys.' I didn't wait for them to say anything. I was afraid they wouldn't, and I would be setting myself up for more pain. The next two nights the same thing happened – no response. I almost gave up doing this. The fourth night I went through the same thing with Jimmy, but this time he didn't roll over. He looked at me. When I finished praying I started to go to Billy's bed when Jimmy reached out, grabbed me and said, 'Can I pray too?' I said, "Sure Jimmy". Here is what he said, 'Dear God, I want to be good. Help me be good. Amen.'

I wanted to stay there and enjoy the moment, but I didn't. I stood up and went to Billy's bed and knelt down and prayed with him. As soon as I was done Billy said, 'Thanks God.'

"Jon, I echoed that prayer. I started to leave the room, and as I was going through the doorway I said, 'Love you guys' and together both boys said, 'Love you Dad.' I could not contain myself. I ran back to Jimmy's bed and picked him up. With Jimmy in one arm, I went to Billy's bed, reached down with my other arm and pulled him out of bed. I stood there hugging my boys, crying like a baby. Jon, my boys love me, and they called me 'Dad'."

This formerly depressed father demonstrated to his boys a picture of what God is like. Scott not only won them to the Lord, the Lord drew the boys to their dad. In a very short time Scott had the honor of leading them to Christ. I'll never forget the tears of joy running down his face as he related his story. What a wonderful sight to see a man humble himself! God gives power to the man who is humble. God truly blessed Scott for dying to himself and living for his Lord Jesus. Hey, good coaching Scott. Both your boys hit a home run, and God helped you win the game.

The Daughter Got Her Mom Out Of Prison

Our heart breaks when we hear that a single parent, who was in post partum depression, took the innocent life of her infant daughter. She could not live with the guilt and wanted to die. What do you tell her? The Bible has the answer, and she chose to believe God.

I met Allen and Jane in California. When Jane was a single parent she used her own hands to take the life of her infant daughter. After years of being in a physical prison made of block walls, steel cells, and surrounded with tall wire fences she was released. Now on the outside of those walls, she found she was in a prison without walls. This prison was the bondage of guilt that the sentence and the prison with walls did not remove.

After being released from prison with the requirement to get psychological treatment, Jane met and married Allen, a Christian man who knew what Jane had done. Allen loved her and wanted to help her heal. He soon discovered that Jane was suicidal, and their marriage seemed doomed from the beginning. Allen thought her problem was only a psychological one, so he tried to help her on that level by taking her to one clinic after another. Even though Allen was a Christian man he didn't know the significance of the scripture in II Cor 6:14 "Don't be teamed with those who do not love the Lord, for what do the people of God have in common with the people of sin? How can light live with darkness?"

To Jane there was no way out of this prison without walls. When I met this couple, Jane had no hope. Therefore, I went through the plan of salvation with her, and she saw that Jesus held the keys to freedom. God wanted her to experience freedom from the guilt that was driving her to suicide. Jesus paid the full price for the sins of everyone who ever lived. This good news overwhelmed her, and with great joy Jane put her trust in Jesus to be her Savior and Lord.

I told Jane, "What you just did is the first of two things God calls all of us to do. The second step will free you from the legitimate guilt you are experiencing. I opened the Bible to Acts 24:16 "And herein do I exercise myself, to have always a conscience void of offence toward God, and *toward* men." (KJV)

I said, "By asking Jesus to come into your life to forgive your sins, you have done what God required. Now you can ask your daughter to forgive you. Jane exclaimed, "How can I do that? It's too late! I killed my daughter." I asked if she had given the little girl a name. She said her name was Phyllis.

I told her, "The Bible tells us where Phyllis is. There is a story in the Bible about David whose infant son died. David asked in 11Sam 12:23b ...."Can I bring him back again? I shall go to him, but he shall not return to me." (NKJV) David knew that his child went to heaven, and when David died, he too would go to heaven to be with him. Therefore, Phyllis is in heaven. She saw Jesus face to face, and she has become like Him, for it says in ICor 13:12 "but then face to face: now I know in part; but then shall I know even as also I am known." (KJV)

Phyllis knows the end from the beginning just like Jesus, because now she is like Him. Your daughter knows even as she is known. She also knows what Acts 24:16 says, and she wants you to be free of guilt. Your daughter knows that when you have a clear conscience you will be able to make right decisions consistently. I encouraged Jane to call her sin by its worst name so there would be nothing left over for her to admit.

In tears, Jane, a brand new Christian, called out to her Father in heaven. Jane asked Him to bring Phyllis to His side. With Phyllis by His side, Jane said, I'm so sorry for choking you. I was wrong for having murdered you with my own hands. I don't deserve to live. Jesus just gave me new life, and now I can ask you to forgive me. Will you forgive me, Phyllis?" With the spiritual assurance that her daughter did forgive her, Jane sobbed as she thanked God, and her daughter for receiving her repentance. From Phyllis's position in heaven, she wanted her Mom to know that she understood the flesh is weak, but the spirit is strong. It's as though Jane could hear her daughter say, "Mom, you are washed as white as snow, justified – just as if you had never sinned."

Jane had real peace on her face and in her heart. The blood of Jesus washed her sins away when He died on the cross. Jane was free from the prison without walls.

You might be thinking – that's all Jane needs to do? She murdered her child!

Rom 1:15 says, "They are quick to kill, hating anyone who disagrees with them. Then verse 22 says, ".... Now God says he will accept and acquit us—declare us "not guilty"—if we trust Jesus Christ to take away our sins. And we all can be saved in the same way."

The only unpardonable sin in the Bible is when a person rejects Jesus as his or her Savior and Lord. When you reject

Jesus, you reject God's sacrifice to pardon every one of us. The good news is recorded right here and in many other places in the Bible. None of us deserves what God lovingly chose to offer us as per the death of His Son. Romans 3:23 says "All have sinned and fall short of the glory of God. We can all say, "Thank you Jesus."

22ⁿᵈ Inning

In The Locker Room

I met with three guys on my team who didn't know for whom they were playing the game of life and they were suffering the natural consequences. I met Jim, Jack, and Bob individually on three separate occasions in the locker room during the game. I explained that they would improve if they quit playing the game for a set of human parents or for a human boss who umpires in this ballpark of opposition and frustration. Each was having a struggle obeying authority in their lives. Let's see how they played their position this inning after we talked.

Jim came with me to the locker room first and told me that he did fine with his mom, but he and his Dad clashed all the time. I asked him to give me an example.

Jim said, "One evening I was watching my favorite TV program. My dad was reading the paper, not paying any attention to what I was watching. Right at the most exciting part of the show Dad said, 'Jim, empty the garbage.' I simply said, "Dad, this is the best part of the show." Dad didn't even look up from his newspaper but yelled out, 'now!!!' "You see what I mean Jon. It really gets me in the pit of my stomach. I'm in my last year of high school. Why do I have to empty the garbage all the time?" I asked Jim, "Do you have a date this weekend?" Jim said, "Yes, I'm going out Saturday night."

I asked, "Jim, do you have a car?"

He said he borrows his Dad's car.

I asked, "Isn't it pretty hard to ask your Dad for the keys to the car when you are at odds with him all the time?"

Jim said, "Yes it is. I have to mow the lawn, polish his shoes and all kinds of junk, so he'll let me have the car just before it's time to leave to pick up my date."

I said, "How would you like to have your Dad throw you the keys to the car?"

Jim laughed and said, "That will never happen. Why do you assume he'll throw me the keys to the car? Have you met my Dad?"

I said, "No."

Jim asked, "Then why do you believe he would do that?"

I said, "Because I'm a Dad."

Jim said, "OK, I give up. What am I supposed to do?"

I surprised Jim by saying, "Never obey your Dad again."

I paused and Jim said, "I won't ever get the car if I do that!"

I said, "Sure you will. Who do you believe speaks through authority?"

Jim said, "God speaks through authority."

I said, "Yes! Therefore, when your Dad says, 'empty the garbage', who is asking you?"

Jim said, "God is asking me to empty the garbage?"

I said, "Jim, you will do a lot more for God than you ever will for your Dad. Bypass your Dad and empty the garbage for Jesus. After all, it's Jesus who will pay you." Jim said, "What?" I said, "Look at this in Col 3:22-25 "You slaves (Jim) must always obey your earthly masters (Dad), not only trying to please them when they are watching you but all the time; obey them willingly because of your love for the Lord and because you want to please him. Work hard and cheerfully at all you do, just as though you were working for the Lord and not merely for your masters, remembering that it is the Lord Christ who is going to pay you, giving you your full portion of all he owns. He is the one you are really working for. And if you don't do your best for him, he will pay you in a way that you won't like—for he has no special favorites who can get away with shirking." (TLB)

Romans 13:1-3 says the same thing. "Let every soul be subject to the governing authorities. (Dad) For there is no authority except from God, and the authorities that exist are appointed by God. Therefore whoever resists the authority resists the ordinance of God, and those who resist will bring judgment on themselves. (In your case Jim, you get no keys to the car!) For rulers are not a terror to good works, but to evil. Do you want to be unafraid of the authority? Do what is good and you will have praise from the same." (NKJV) If we don't play the game according to God's game plan, you will suffer the consequences."

Jim said, "OK, but what I'm doing is important to me. Doesn't that count for anything?"

I said, "Lord means 'Boss'. Jump up and say, 'OK, Dad.' Take off, and do what Jesus asked you to do through your Dad. Then come back, and ask your Dad if there is anything else he wants you to do."

Jim left with the game plan right out of the Bible. One week later Jim came over again.

He asked me, "Did you call my Dad?"

I said, "No. What happened?"

Jim said, "Dad threw me the keys to the car on Saturday morning. I had the car all day, and for the date that night. I couldn't believe it. Jon, this should have been on Candid Camera. He asked me to do something, like always, at a most inconvenient time, but I jumped up and said, 'OK,

Dad' I raced out of the room and did it. I came back in, and there was Dad, with the paper crunched in his lap starring at the floor. It was a beautiful sight. Then something happened that you mentioned. Dad was mean to me for the next few days supposing that I was playing a little mind game with him. I continued doing things for Jesus, and by Friday Dad asked me to do something in a normal conversational tone. I couldn't believe it. Saturday morning at breakfast, Dad threw me the keys to the car."

I heard months later that Jim kept it up, and he had a great senior year and summer. He contacted me his freshman year after his first semester break from college. He said, "Jon, I'm back home from college, and I had another encounter with Dad." I asked what happened. Jim said, "When will I get rid of having to empty the garbage, I'm a college man now? This is ridiculous. When is this going to end?" I said, "That's easy; when you get married." Jim said, "Then my wife will ask me to empty the garbage." I said, "I can see it now. You and your wife have a baby in a year or two. Five years following that you look at your five year old child and say, 'empty the garbage.' That's how you get rid of the job. When she goes off to college, you will have to empty the garbage again. You have only a few brief years to be free from that job. Of course, you could keep on having children to whom you could give that job.

This same scripture also worked for a Christian employee named Jack. He worked at a big manufacturing company, and Jack's foreman hated Christians. The foreman gave Jack a lot of grief. His boss would swear using the Lord's name. He used many other swear words as he instructed Jack to sweep the third aisle. Jack took those instructions, as though they came from Jesus and enjoyed the rewards that came as the Lord honored Jack's labor for Him. In just a few weeks his boss gave Jack a raise and a promotion. God honors His game plan. Here again, the Lord is not so concerned with what is happening to us as He is with how we respond to it. The boss may have meant it for evil, but God used it for good in Jack's life.

Who are the human umpires that God has placed in charge of your game of life? Do they make some unusual and irritating calls against you? How do you respond to those human umpires?

Where did this CEO come from?

Bob had lost hope. He worked for his dad in a big company. Even though he was the top salesman in the company, Bob's dad also gave him low-level jobs to do, such as sweeping the floors, and cleaning the restrooms. Bob hoped that one day, he would be the CEO of the company. Why was his dad putting him through this humiliation? Didn't his dad realize how Bob felt? Did he even care?

Bob came to me with his problem. I asked him if he knew Jesus in a personal way, and he said that he became a Christian in his youth. I asked if his dad was a Christian. Bob stated that he was not only a Christian, but also he was considered a spiritual leader in the community.

I asked Bob for whom he was working, and he said, "My dad." I stated that it was too bad that he worked for his dad. I said to Bob, "You are expecting special treatment from your dad and when you don't get that kind of treatment it eats you alive, and you are becoming bitter.

I asked Bob if he thought he was bitter. He didn't think he was, so I told him that any time you think of something or someone, and it causes pain to your mind, you're bitter. Bob admitted that it was painful to even think about his dad, so he would try to get him out of his mind. I also explained that the one you allow to control your emotions is your god. I said. "Letting a god, especially one you don't like, control your emotion doesn't make a lot of sense, does it?" I told

Bob I heard a good definition for bitterness since it can bring on negative physical affects. I said, "Bitterness is like taking poison and expecting the other person to die." He laughed and agreed that he was bitter. Bob determined to stop taking this self-induced poison.

I said, "If you were working for a non Christian you would have to view God instructing you through that non Christian. How would you work for him? Quit working for your dad, and work for a Christian brother who just happens to be your dad. It's easier to take instruction from God through a Christian brother. God is the One giving you these jobs through authority. There is a stigma of high expectations because you haven't separated your dad from your dad being a Christian brother. You can always quit, but you will go across town, and find yourself working for another authority through whom God will instruct you. Who do you want to work for, your dad or God?

Bob said, "I never looked at it like that. I feel better already. I want to work for God."

What was the result after Bob started working for God through his Christian brother? The change in Bob's work ethic was so good and evident, Bob not only received a raise, he was promoted, and moved right up the ladder. Bob became the sales manager within the year. The CEO title was right around the corner. I've said this before, "Jesus is never in a hurry, but He is always on time."

For whom are you working? Do you hear God telling you what to do through your authority? This can actually take the work out of work. Jim, Jack and Bob did very well. I trust you will too.

If you are the authority, how are you exercising it? Do you make it a joy, for those under you, to work for Jesus?

23rd Inning

This Game Went 'Ten' Innings

Do you know where you are going when you die? Larry and Wendy were counting on keeping the Ten Commandments to get them to heaven. See what they discovered and how they know for sure they will go to heaven. Now, they have no doubts. Do you have doubts?

I met Larry and Wendy in Ohio. Both had been married before and were having marriage problems in this marriage. They shared with me how they met, and how much they loved each other, yet they were beginning to verbally abuse one another.

I asked them if they both knew where they would go if they died today.

Larry and Wendy said in unison, "We would go to heaven."

I said, "Great! What would you say to God if He asked you this question? 'Why should I let you into my heaven?'"

They looked at each other and again said in unison, "We have kept the ten commandments."

I asked, "Do you know the ten commandments?" Larry said, "Sure. You should not murder, you should not steal, and you should go to church." Then he paused and said, while glancing at Wendy, "Isn't there a commandment not to covet somebody else's mate?" He smiled at Wendy and me, and said, "I guess we didn't do too well on that one." They both laughed. Then I asked if they knew any more commandments. They looked at each other, and said, "No, that's about it."

I said, "Let's take inventory. You know four of the Ten Commandments, and you violated one of those. You admit you don't know the other six, and yet you said you are going to get into heaven because you kept the Ten Commandments. How would you know if you're keeping the other six if you don't know what they are?"

Larry and Wendy threw their heads back and laughed.

I asked if they knew why God gave the Ten Commandments.

They didn't know.

I said, "To prove we couldn't keep them. You see, they were written on stone, and the people in the Old Testament time didn't have the Holy Spirit inside them to enable them keep the commandments."

They looked dismayed and asked, "Then how does anyone get into heaven?"

I told them that God had a different way that enables us to enter heaven.

They looked at each other and said, "What has this to do with our marriage problems?"

I said, "Problems can be a good thing. We see that something is wrong, and we can't fix it. We might go to God and discover that His answer does work. He's the only One who can help us with these problems.

Let me show you from scripture what I mean. Rom3:20-25 says, "Now do you see it? No one can ever be made right in God's sight by doing what the law commands. For the more we know of God's laws, the clearer it becomes that we aren't obeying them; his laws serve only to make us see that we are sinners. But now God has shown us a different way to heaven — not by "being good enough" and trying to keep his laws, but by a new way (though not new, really, for the Scriptures told about it long ago). Now God says he will accept and acquit us—declare us "not guilty "—if we trust Jesus Christ to take away our sins. And we all can be saved in this same way, by coming to Christ, no matter who we are or what we have been like. Yes, all have sinned; all fall short of God's glorious ideal; yet now God declares us "not guilty" of offending him if we trust in Jesus Christ, who in his kindness freely takes away our sins. For God sent Christ Jesus to take the punishment for our sins and to end all God's anger against us. He used Christ's blood and our faith as the means of saving us from his wrath." (TLB)

I asked, "Do you have to work for a gift?"

They said, "No."

I told them that God loved them enough to send His Son Jesus to take our place on the cross to shed His blood to wash away our sins. That proved God's love for us. The gift He is offering to everyone is the gift of eternal life. God paid for the gift and leaves it up to us to receive this gift. Can you imagine not wanting a gift like that?

I mentioned that at Christmas time, there are gifts under the Christmas tree, and some of them have your names on them. I can't imagine you walking away saying, 'No thanks."

I said, "There is another tree that has a gift under it with your name on it. That tree is the cross. Being Holy, God could not allow sin into His heaven; therefore, He gave His very life, to wash your sins away. When you see that Jesus loved you enough to pay for your gift with his life, it magnifies the value of the gift. I can't imagine you walking away saying, 'No thanks."

John 1:12 "As many as received Him (Jesus) to them He gave the right to become children of God." (TLB) It says in I John 5:10-13 "All who believe this know in their hearts that it is true. If anyone doesn't believe this, he is actually calling God a liar because he doesn't believe what God has said about his Son. And what is it that God has said? That he has given us eternal life and that this life is in his Son. So whoever has God's Son has life; whoever does not have his Son, does not have life. I have written this to you who believe in the Son of God so that you may **know** you have eternal life." (TLB)

They were both humbled. They had never heard anything like this and would not have believed it had I not read it from the Bible. After I went through the complete plan of salvation, as written in previous chapters of this book, Larry and Wendy trusted Jesus Christ as their own personal Savior and Lord.

Yes, it's all about Jesus. He changes lives. Has He changed your life? Are you telling others who will listen, about what Jesus has done and is doing in your life? Are you telling them how much you appreciate and enjoy the gift of eternal life that He paid for on that cruel cross?

24th Inning

Sacrifice This Inning

Being a dad and mom has to be one of the most difficult tasks given to mankind. They cannot see inside the hearts and minds of their children. God is the only One who can. Parents need His help when raising their children.

In Florida I met Bill, a dad who was really down in the dumps because of his son, Phillip. Phillip had tremendous ability to play tennis, and was awarded an athletic scholarship from a big university. Bill was heartsick when he found out that Phillip had been on drugs since high school and couldn't get off them. Phillip eventually lost his scholarship, even though he had been in four rehabilitation centers that cost Bill big bucks.

Bill's question to me was, "Jon, my wife, and I don't know how far to go. Phillip will always be our son, so we can't just turn our back on him, and yet, he doesn't seem to care about all we have done to try to assist him. We can't just send him away. We don't know what to do!"

I asked Bill if he knew where he was going when he died.

He asked, "What does that have to do with what I'm to do with my son?"

I told him that it had everything to do with his son. I told Bill to answer my question, and I would show him how it applied to Phillip.

Bill said, "First of all, no one knows where they are going when they die. You just have to wait until you get there and hope for the best. I assume I will get into heaven, because I haven't hurt anyone, and God knows I've tried to do good all my life."

I asked Bill if what he believed about getting into heaven were not true, would he want to know it. He told me, "God is a loving God, so why wouldn't He let me in?"

Again, I asked Bill, "If what you believe right now, about getting into heaven, is not true, would you want to know it?"

He said, "Sure. I would be an idiot to hang on to what isn't true. Tell me what is the truth, and why I should believe your opinion of what is true?

I said, "You gave me your opinion. Everyone has an opinion. I also have opinions, but I would rather give you what God told us in His Word, the Bible, so we can know what the truth is from God Himself. Looking at life from God's point of view is called wisdom. I can trust what He said through holy men of old who were inspired by God the Holy Spirit.

Bill wanted to know the truth; therefore, I shared with him the gospel, and he was quick to accept Jesus Christ to be his Savior and Lord.

After he prayed he said, "Now I believe I'm going to heaven when I die. That's good for me, but you said that my knowing the truth would have everything to do with Phillip. I don't get it."

I said, "Bill, you just gave your life to Jesus Christ. You must have trusted Him with your life, or you wouldn't have given it to him, right?" Bill agreed. I said, "Since you trusted Jesus with your life, you can now trust Jesus with your son's life! You would not have been able to do that before you trusted the Lord Jesus with your own life."

I said, "A few moments ago you told me you didn't know what to do with Phillip."

Bill said, "Oh, I get it. When I give Phillip to the Lord, I can trust the Lord to get the truth to my son just like He got the truth to me. Will you talk to Phillip?"

I said, "Sure. However, he may not want to speak with me. You might be the one the Lord will use to share this good news with your son. You chose to believe the truth, and the truth has set you free. If Phillip chooses to believe, like you just did, he will be set free as well. You can give Phillip to the Lord, and trust God to get through to him. It will be up to Phillip to be open to the Lord. By giving Phillip to the Lord, you are doing what Abraham did as he gave his son Isaac to God. Giving someone you love is a great sacrifice, and the Father in heaven knows how difficult that can be, for He gave His son Jesus for our salvation. The story about Abraham is one with which you can identify.

It's found in Gen 22:1-14 "Later on, God tested Abraham's faith and obedience. "Abraham!" God called. "Yes, Lord?" he replied. "Take with you your only son—yes, Isaac whom you love so much—and go to the land of Moriah and sacrifice him there as a burnt offering upon one of the mountains which I'll point out to you!" The next morning Abraham got up early, chopped wood for a fire upon the altar, saddled his donkey, and took with him his son Isaac and two young men who were his servants, and started off to the place where God had told him to go. On the third day of the journey Abraham saw the place in the distance. "Stay here with the donkey," Abraham told the young men, "and the lad and I will travel yonder and worship, and then come right back." Abraham placed the wood for the burnt offering upon Isaac's shoulders, while he himself carried the knife and the flint for striking a fire. So the two of them went on together. "Father,"

Isaac asked, "we have the wood and the flint to make the fire, but where is the lamb for the sacrifice?" "God will see to it, my son," Abraham replied. And they went on. When they arrived at the place where God had told Abraham to go, he built an altar and placed the wood in order, ready for the fire, and then tied Isaac and laid him on the altar over the wood. And Abraham took the knife and lifted it up to plunge it into his son, to slay him. At that moment the Angel of God shouted to him from heaven, "Abraham! Abraham!" "Yes, Lord!" he answered. "Lay down the knife; don't hurt the lad in any way," the Angel said, "for I know that God is first in your life—you have not withheld even your beloved son from me." Then Abraham noticed a ram caught by its horns in a bush. So he took the ram and sacrificed it, instead of his son, as a burnt offering on the altar. Abraham named the place "Jehovah provides"—and it still goes by that name to this day." (TLB)

"It's a real sacrifice to give up a loved one. But, to whom are you giving Phillip? You are trusting God to draw your son to Himself. God is not willing that anyone perishes. You are giving Phillip to the only One who can save him. Now, can you see how your salvation had to come first before you could trust the Lord with Phillip's life?

I suggested to Bill that he could give Phillip to God right now. Bill didn't hesitate. He bowed his head and said, "God, I just trusted you with my life. I now trust you with my son Phillip. I'm sure you can draw him to Jesus like you drew me. Help me show my son that you are the truth, and he needs you in his life. Thanks God."

I asked Bill, "Can you see how God used your son and his problems to show you your need for Jesus? God may use the change in your life to reach Phillip.

After reading this story, can you see how important it is to give your life to God in order to be able to give your loved ones to God? The Father in Heaven sacrificed His Son so we could have eternal life. It is not a sacrifice for us to give our children to God. We give them to God because He can take care of His property better than we treat our own property.

I hope that these real life situations have a positive effect on you and on those the Lord touches through your life.

25th Inning

A 'Bully' Lost This Inning

Have you ever been bullied? What did you do about it? Sometimes there is nothing else to do but stand up against them. Cole was faced with Billy the bully, and he didn't know what else to do but avoid Billy, so he stayed home from school. Cole's mother Tracey brought him to talk to me, and I shared two true stories with Cole. The bully is still there, but Cole was set free.

The first story I shared with Cole was about an evangelist who had a son named Dean. They had moved to a different city, and Dean was enrolled in one of the local schools. Monday morning he left for school and was stopped just a few blocks from home by the local bully and his buddies. They had been waiting for this 'new kid' on the block. They were going to show Dean that this big bully was the one you were to follow if you knew what was good for you.

Billy the bully stepped in front of Dean as the others watched. Dean was scared to death and believed he was going to get clobbered. Dean looked into the bully's eyes; in his mind and heart he was saying, "Lord, I'm about to be destroyed. I'm scared, and I need your help. I don't know what to do. He's twice as big as I am."

Billy looked at Dean, and Billy's piercing eyes were telling Dean that he was the top dog in this neighborhood. You better fall in line or you answer to me. After this long standoff stare something happened that totally took Dean by surprise. All of a sudden, Billy put his arm around Dean and walked him to the playground and introduced Dean to everyone saying, "This is the toughest kid I ever met." God answered Dean's prayer. Do you pray on the spot? It takes practice. You don't need a bully facing you to learn how to pray in season and out of season.

The next story I told Cole and Tracy was about my son Lee.

"Lee was a freshman in high school, and while sitting in study hall, he felt the sharp point of a knife stick him in the back. Joe was a senior who sat behind Lee. Joe told Lee to grab the rear of the girl he pointed out as she left the room. In fear, Lee did as he was told, and the girl swung at Lee, but she missed.

Lee came home and told me the whole story. Lee was afraid that Joe would tell him to do something else to that girl or some other girl the next day. I asked Lee what Joe used on him, and Lee said, 'a knife.' I asked Lee, "Why don't you use the sword on him." Lee looked surprised. He asked me what I meant. I told Lee that another name for the Bible is, 'The sword'. I suggested that Lee drop the 4 Spiritual Laws, a clear, Biblical presentation of salvation, on Joe's desk, and ask him to read it.

The next day Lee did just that. Joe said he would read the tract. The following day Lee asked Joe if he had read the Four Spiritual Laws. Joe said that he had, and Lee asked him if he had prayed the prayer near the end of the tract. Joe said that he did pray the prayer, and he thanked Lee for giving the tract to him.

A short time later Lee was in the boy's restroom when another tough guy began making fun of Lee for brushing his teeth. Lee had braces, and the doctor's order was that he brush his teeth after each meal. This new bully was having a lot of fun teasing Lee when Joe came into the restroom and saw what was going on. Joe yelled out, "Hey! Knock it off! Lee's my man." Joe became Lee's personal bodyguard instead of bullying him the rest of the year. What a huge turnaround that was. Lee uses the 'sword' to this very day.

I asked Cole if he knew where he was going when he died. If a person knows he will go to heaven when he dies, the fear of death goes out the window. If one takes care of the future, he is better equipped to deal with the present.

Both Cole and his mom, Tracy asked Jesus Christ into their lives. What will follow their decision to trust Jesus can be related to the Biblical account of Jesus and Nicodemus, found in the third chapter of the book of John, 'that which is born of flesh is flesh; that which is born of the spirit is spirit.' This statement indicates a spiritual birth. A physical baby coming into the world does not, all of a sudden, become a full grown adult. The same is true with a baby Christian. The physical baby must be fed milk and eventually solid food in order to grow and become strong. The Word of God, known as 'milk', will feed the Spiritual baby as we read in I Cor 3:1-2 "Dear brothers, I have been talking to you as though you were still just babies in the Christian life who are not following the Lord but your own desires; I cannot talk to you as I would to healthy Christians who are filled with the Spirit.

I have had to feed you with milk and not with solid food because you couldn't digest anything stronger. And even now you still have to be fed on milk." (TLB)

It will require some time to grow in the Lord to be able to look at 'Billy the Bully' straight in the eye and respond as Christ would. I repeat, 'a conversion to Christ does not make one an immediate spiritual adult.' Reading the Word of God, and using the strength that comes from it, will help us do what the Word says to do. We will begin to experience a quiet growth in grace and character.

Cole and Tracy have a long way to go, but they could not have had the assurance of the Lord's help apart from receiving Him into their lives.

When you are faced with a bully, what do you think you will do? Do you have Jesus in your heart to direct you on the spot? Will you pray immediately when faced with a bully? Over the years God has given many people extra innings to get right with Him. What inning are you in right now? Play as though it's the last inning, and you will finish the game well. By the way, you're not a bully, are you?

26th Inning

This Inning Was On 'Radio' and 'TV'

God has used different experiences to get the attention of many people in order to show them a clear picture of salvation. He uses the illustration of a radio and TV to show that we must be on His frequency to get the picture he wants to show us. Again, God uses everything for His own use and glory. Watch how He uses light, warmth, radio, TV, clouds, and ridicule to draw people to Himself.

You cannot watch the game on radio, but you can hear and watch a sporting event on TV. I gave a seminar in Michigan and a couple, Tom and Sally asked me to have dinner one evening before that night's seminar session. Near the end of the meal, Tom wanted to tell me about his spiritual experience. I always like to hear testimonies, so I encouraged him to tell me his story. The expression on his face seemed uncertain, and Tom said he had never told anyone this before.

Tom said, "I saw a beautiful bright light at the foot of my bed one night that made me feel like I must be a Christian. Although I had this supernatural experience I felt that if I told anyone they might think I was out of my mind." I asked, "Is the reason you asked me to come over tonight because you have doubts that you're really are a Christian?" He said, "Yes. I definitely needed a spiritual leader to hear my story and explain why I have these doubts.

I said that God is free to allow or cause an experience to get our attention so that we will pursue God's way of salvation. I said, "I believe God allowed you to have that supernatural experience, but I also think you will have difficulty leading people to salvation with that experience. For example, you are talking with someone about spiritual things, and you see that they are ready to get right with God. You then tell them that all they have to do is to look down at the foot of their bed each night for a beautiful bright light. When they see such a light, they will be assured that they are Christians. You will have difficulty witnessing like this for three reasons. One, you personally have 'God given' doubts yourself. Two, you are not sure they will have an experience like you did, because you haven't heard of anyone else having this experience, and three, you doubt that you could really lead anyone to Christ using your experience to save them."

I continued, "I believe what you really want is salvation and the assurance that follows so you can tell others that they can have assurance as well. He said, "That's it!"

I used an illustration about how God can use a 'radio' and a 'tv' to explain the difference between a person on his way to hell and the person going to heaven. I said, "Picture me being born into this world as a radio. The sounds of people talking and music playing came through me. There was nothing wrong with me. I was a fine radio. I picked up radio frequencies. People listened to me.

One day I heard that radios go to hell. I was so disappointed and wondered, 'Then who goes to heaven?' I heard about television. You could actually see and hear the people speaking and watch and hear the people playing their musical instruments. What a great upgrade. I learned that a 'tv set' goes to heaven.

As a radio, I noticed I could not pick up a TV frequency. I tried and tried but that frequency went right over my head and didn't come through my radio. I also noticed that the TV could not pick up my radio frequency. Not being on the same frequency, the TV and I could not understand one another.

Since I heard that a radio goes to hell but a TV goes to heaven, I wanted to find out how I could be 'converted' to a TV. I tried on my own and thought I had it figured out when I saw a bright light one evening, but it was just a wire that came loose making a spark that caused the bright light to appear. I must be wearing out and dying. However, a bright light was used to get my attention. Just how long would I last before I would go to hell?

Then I heard some really good news. I heard that every TV used to be a radio. I was told that the Creator of the radio could convert the radio into a TV, giving the 'TV' assurance of going to heaven.

A non Christian is like that 'radio'. He cannot pick up the frequency of the Christian. They won't understand one another until the non Christian asks the creator, Jesus Christ, into his life. Now a Christian can understand another Christian because they are on the same spiritual frequency.

I asked Tom if he was ready to have Jesus Christ come into his life to convert him into a 'tv' as per this illustration. He understood that the bright light was used of God to get his attention. He followed me in the prayer of salvation and asked Jesus Christ to come into his heart.

Then I turned to Sally, and asked her if she had asked Jesus into her heart. She said, "I just did. I prayed that prayer along with you and Tom. Hey, God used that bright light to bring both the husband and the wife to Christ. God is good.

Illustration: in a different situation.

An adult married daughter and her mother were not on the same frequency. The daughter, Lisa knew that her Mom was not a Christian, but the mother was convinced that she was. Everything the daughter said on the subject went right over her Mother's head. Lisa arranged for her Mother to come in to see me while I was in Nebraska.

I asked the Mother to share with me why she believed she was a Christian. She said she was sitting in her church one Sunday morning, and she had a warm feeling come over her. Her husband died a few years later, and she was at the cemetery where they were about to bury him. She said she looked up and saw a cloud in the form of a cross. She said, "It confirmed in my mind that God was telling me that I was a Christian. Lisa will not look at it from my perspective. We are growing apart because she is so stubborn!"

I asked if she had led anyone to Christ. She said that she did not have the gift of evangelism. I asked what she would tell a person who was asking how to become a Christian? She had no answer; therefore, I asked her if I could give her one. She was curious and asked me to tell her what I had in mind. I said, "All you have to do when you see the secular conversation you are having with someone turn into a spiritual one, is to ask the person if she would like to become a Christian? If she says, 'yes.' then you can tell her, 'go to church next Sunday morning and wait there until you have a warm feeling come over you. Then, when your mate dies, look up in the sky just before they bury your mate to see if a cloud is there in the form of a cross.' You can tell her that this will confirm that she really is a Christian."

This dear lady began to laugh. She said, "That sounds silly, doesn't it?" She never saw how silly it was until she heard it played back as a way to lead someone to Christ. She wanted to have a right relationship with Lisa so they could be close again. I told her that it would even be worse if she never did understand her daughter before she died.

I explained that she could have a great relationship with her daughter and be able to understand Lisa if she would be willing to do what God would have her do first. I shared the story of salvation with her, and she was eager to receive Jesus Christ as her Savior and Lord. Sometime later she came in with Lisa. They were truly on the same frequency. What a joy it was for me to see this Mom and her daughter understand one another and have the closeness they both had longed for. Only God could do such a wonderful thing.

Let me take a minute here and ask you a question. As you are reading this book do you find that you are not relating, and it makes no sense to you?

When a non-Christian reads the Bible it's like reading someone else's mail. The Lord wrote the Bible as a love letter to those who trusted Him. Unless you have received Him into your heart you will not understand the Bible. Once a person has received Jesus into his heart, he has the author of the Bible in his heart and the Holy Spirit will make understanding it possible.

If you are so inclined, pause right here and pray this simple prayer. "Lord Jesus. I am having difficulty understanding this. Jesus, I ask you to come into my heart and be my Savior and Lord. Help me understand what you are saying. I want to be on your frequency. I agree with you that I am a sinner, and I believe you and thank you for dying on the cross to wash my sins away. By faith I thank you for hearing and answering my prayer. I pray this in Jesus name. Amen."

Since we cannot see the future we have to live by faith. Faith is the only thing that pleases God. He has lovingly locked us into pleasing Him. Isn't that wonderful? He loves you. Isn't that great? It's easy to love Him back, isn't it?

27ᵗʰ Inning

Three Great Hits off the 'Opponent'

The 'first' big hit of the inning:

S atan has many pitches in his arsenal to strike you out. If you are not practicing consistently in the batting cage to keep you eye on the ball, improving your stance, timing your swing etc. you will not be ready, during the game, when he throws his pitch. You will strike out. He has many unusual pitches. He has a great junk ball pitch. Let's see what Betty, Carol and Monica did during their time at bat. First, Betty's at bat.

Betty lived in Nashville, Tennessee. She was a single parent with a six-year-old daughter and a fifteen-year-old son. Betty met with me to explain that she saw and heard supernatural things in her home. The house was big enough for the three of them, and the rent was low because no one else would stay there very long. Betty didn't think anything about it until these scary things began to happen.

Betty explained that the drapes in her daughter's room were the kind you had to close and open by hand. Just as Betty was leaving the room, after closing the drapes, they opened by themselves. This happened many times. Also, Betty and the children heard what sounded like a table and chairs being moved across the attic floor. They went up to check and there was no furniture up there. Her son was sleeping one night, when all of a sudden he awoke and noticed figures of people illumined like light at the end of his bed, They were moving and floating back and forth. He threw the covers over his head and told his Mom the next morning. She said, "If you don't bother them, they won't bother you." Betty was afraid to tell any one about this for fear they would assume she was crazy. When Betty turned on the 700 Club Ministry program on TV, she noticed the weird manifestations didn't take place. They were living in fear and could not afford a more expensive place to live.

Another Christian man and I went to the house with Betty at her request. We walked around the boundaries of the property, went into each room of the house, into the attic, and into the basement saying these words. "By the authority of Jesus' name and the power of His blood we command any evil spirits to leave." We felt a bit strange doing this but scripture tells us that being Christians, we can enter into the victory of Christ over the enemy. The scripture says in James 4:7 "Therefore; submit to God, resist the devil, and he will flee from you." (NKJV)

Betty notified us later that her son became a Christian due to the power he saw in Jesus. All the manifestations stopped. Who are we playing against in this major league of life? It says in Eph. 6:12 "For we are not fighting against people made of flesh and blood, but against persons without bodies—the evil rulers of the unseen world, those mighty satanic beings and great evil princes of darkness who rule this world; and against huge numbers of wicked spirits in the spirit world." (TLB)

That was a wicked pitch that Satan threw Betty. Phil. 4:13 says, "but greater is He who is in you than he that is in the world." You are more than conquerors in Christ Jesus.

The 'second' big hit of the inning:

Satan can make you think that what he would have you do is innocent, but is it? Look at the wicked pitch Satan threw at Carol, a sophomore in college. She is a Christian girl that had not been adequately warned and had not spent the amount of time necessary to be able to discern what was being thrown to her when it was her turn to bat. See what affect it had on Carol and what she finally had to do about it.

I was in California with my family giving a seminar when Pat approached me with what she believed to be her last hope before taking her Christian suicidal daughter, Carol, to the hospital. Pat told me that Carol was a sophomore in a Christian college. During Carol's first year she did fine, and was on the Dean's list. Pat said, "We were so happy for her, and felt we had picked just the right Christian school. Three months into Carol's sophomore year we received a call from the school counselor with the tragic news that she had tried to take her own life. Carol had been throwing furniture against the walls of her dorm room. The students next door heard all this noise and rushed into Carol's room to find her holding a piece of broken glass next to her wrist, as though she intended to cut herself. Would you please speak with Carol? We can't get through to her, so we are going to take her to the hospital. Some friends of ours are attending your seminar, and they suggested that we bring Carol to see you. They heard you mention having experiences with similar situations. Jon, Carol is a good Christian girl, and this isn't like her. On top of all this, she told us she hears voices. We don't know you, but our friends have confidence in your background and how you developed your ministry from the Bible."

We set a time for me to meet with Carol that evening and she was eager to talk. Carol didn't want to go to the hospital. One of the first things Carol told me was that she hears a voice.

Carol said, "I hear it right now. He's right here. Can you hear him? I'm scared, Jon."

I asked Carol, "Does he have a name?"

She said, "His name is Otto, and he won't leave me alone."

I asked her, "What was different between your freshman year and the first few months of this year. Carol said, "I had a great roommate my freshman year, but she moved. We were both on the Dean's list. I was looking forward to going back to school my sophomore year to room with her again. I was disappointed when she changed schools to be closer to her parents. Consequently, the school assigned me a new room-mate. Gwen was from a good Christian home; as a matter of fact, her dad's a minister."

Carol continued, "I felt safe and didn't think anything about it when Gwen was reading the daily horoscopes in the newspaper. I assumed that since she is the daughter of a minister that she must not think anything was wrong with that, but I did ask what her dad believed about it. She said, 'Dad wants me to get a good Christian education; he said that nothing can harm me, since I'm a Christian.'

Carol said, "I didn't want to be a 'prude', but I asked, "You had a conviction not to read horoscopes, and you went against your conviction? She said, 'Yes.' If it didn't hurt her, I didn't see how it would hurt me. We became close, because we had this in common. Then one day Gwen suggested that we go to the school library and check out some books that show you how to do weird things. We bought candles, and did the chants we learned about in these books. We were into levitation and all kinds of stuff. This was exciting. One night, when we were playing cards, we put the palms of our hands on the tabletop, and with a statement we learned from the book, we lifted our hands up slowly, and the table came up too. We were shocked and scared, yet exhilarated at the same time. We asked each other, 'Did you use your knees?' to move the table up; we had not. We did it again. We went back to the library to get more cult books and tried other stuff."

She continued, "Gwen suggested, 'Let's try some beer. A lot of the other kids are doing it, and they seem to be having fun. I've been a PK all my life, and I just want to see what it tastes like.' We started drinking, and sometimes we got drunk. We were both virgins, but one day we lost our convictions about that too. The first time I had sex, I felt sick, but Gwen reminded me about how sick I got the first time I was drunk. She said it was the same thing."

I asked Carol if she was ready to trust Jesus to free her from Otto and his voice.

Carol said, "Yes, but I don't know how. Jesus must be disgusted with me by now. I'm afraid I'm going crazy. My parents believe I'm going to end up in the mental ward. I know my parents love me, and I love them. I can't believe this has happened to me, especially in a Christian college and with a Christian roommate."

I told Carol that she would have to go back in her heart and mind to where she first said no to God and renounce what she did at that time.

She said, "Where do I start?"

I said, "When did you first said no to God?"

She said, "When I became a people pleaser instead of obeying God's still small voice."

I showed Carol the story about David and Uriah.

II Sam 11:17 "It happened in the spring of the year, at the time when kings go out *to battle,* that David sent Joab and his servants with him, and all Israel; and they destroyed the people of Ammon and besieged Rabbah. But David remained at Jerusalem. *(This is when he "first" said no to God)* Then it happened one evening that David arose from his bed and walked on the roof of the king's house. And from the roof he saw a woman bathing, and the woman *was* very beautiful to behold. So David sent and inquired about the woman. And *someone* said, "*Is* this not Bathsheba, the daughter of Eliam, the wife of Uriah the Hittite?" Then David sent messengers, and took her; and she came to him, and he lay with her, *(This is his "second" time saying no to God. He already had all of Saul's wives.)* for she was cleansed from her impurity; and she returned to her house. And the woman conceived; so she sent and told David, and said, "I *am* with child." Then David sent to Joab, *saying,* "Send me Uriah the Hittite." And Joab sent Uriah to David. When Uriah had come to him, David asked how Joab was doing, and how the people were doing, and how the war prospered. And David said to Uriah, "Go down to your house and wash your feet." So Uriah departed from the king's house, and a gift *of food* from the king followed him. But Uriah slept at the door of the king's house with all the servants of his lord, and did not go down to his house. So when they told David, saying, "Uriah did not go down to his house," David said to Uriah, "Did you not come from a journey? Why did you not go down to your house?" And Uriah said to David, "The ark and Israel and Judah are dwelling in tents, and my lord Joab and the servants of my lord are encamped in the open fields. Shall I then go to my house to eat and drink, and to lie with my wife? *As* you live, and *as* your soul lives, I will not do this thing." Then David said to Uriah, "Wait here today also, and tomorrow I will let you depart." So Uriah remained in Jerusalem that day and the next. Now when David called him, he ate and drank before him; and he made him drunk. And at evening he went out to lie on his bed with the servants of his lord, but he did not go down to his house. In the morning it happened that David wrote a letter to Joab and sent *it* by the hand of Uriah. And he wrote in the letter, saying, "Set Uriah in the forefront of the hottest battle, and retreat from him, that he may be struck down and die." *(Murder was David's "third" major disobedient sinful act because he was powerless. You cannot make consistent right decisions without having a clear conscience.)* So it was, while Joab besieged the city, that he assigned Uriah to a place where he knew there *were* valiant men. Then the men of the city came out and fought with Joab. And *some* of the people of the servants of David fell; and Uriah the Hittite died also." (NKJV)

I stepped Carol through each thing she knew was wrong; being a people pleaser, checking out cult books, drinking, giving her body to guys etc. Carol said, "Jon, I don't hear Otto's voice. He's gone. She smiled for the first time in our conversation.

Carol followed me in prayer, "Dear Father in heaven, I have sinned against you by trying to see the future in horoscopes. I went against the conviction of my spirit and your Word. By the authority of Jesus name and the power of His blood, I renounce and rebuke any transference of satanic power which is affecting me now."

There is so much more, but suffice it to say, we don't have the freedom to say no to God, or we are asking for the natural consequences that could be extremely severe. Carol also experienced the joy of being obedient to the Lord and drawing upon His mercy and forgiveness that gave her a new lease on life.

Palm readings at a carnival, horoscopes, etc. seem so innocent and fun to try. Satan is a master at tweaking our lower nature to get us to do our own thing. Have you dabbled in the occult or know of others that have? I hope these first two hits help you see that Satan wants you to play God and tell Him what and when you are going to do something He forbids. Satan can 'pitch' you thoughts and the scripture says in II Cor 10:5 says, "casting down imaginations and every high thing that exalts itself against the knowledge of God, and bringing every thought into captivity to the obedience of Christ." (NKJV)" Unless you hit these thoughts where they belong you will strike out. Keep you eye on that pitch, see the 'spin', and time your swing. God will give you the contact you need. Where the ball goes is God's choice. He is in control of this game. He put Carol back in the game. I'm sure she will spend more time in the batting cage hitting pitches.

Watch what Satan's thoughts (pitches) did to Monica and see the third hit of the inning.

The 'third' big hit of the inning:

Do you bring every thought (pitch) into captivity and the obedience of Christ? Monica didn't know what was happening until she felt there was no way out but to quit the game by taking her own life. There is a scriptural plan to save her life and get her back in the line up. She was obedient, and God is faithful.

The real enemy is alive and well. Satan wants Christians to say no to God, because he knows that God chastens every one of His own. Satan loves it when we get spanked for not seeing who the enemy really is and suckered in by the thoughts he can give us.

Monica became suicidal because of the guilt she was experiencing with her husband. He didn't have a clue that his wife was so miserable. She knew her misery was all her fault; therefore she couldn't tell him.

When they would be engaged in normal physical relations with each other, Monica was not experiencing the normal satisfaction that should take place. Monica noticed that she was able to satisfy her husband, but she could not tell him that he was not bringing her satisfaction.

The real enemy was able to put a thought in her mind that did bring her to the same physical satisfaction that her husband was experiencing. Her guilt came from knowing that it was not her husband bringing her the normal pleasure of marriage. She said, "I can't tell him. It would break his heart."

She felt guilty from drawing upon the enemy's thoughts and guilty for withholding the truth from her husband. The guilt from either one of these things made her suicidal, so she came to me in hopes of getting a Biblical answer.

I told her a story I heard from a wonderful Christian leader. He knew of a man who had a terrible time with pornography, drugs, alcohol etc. and was so out of it that the hospital had given up on him for not responding to any of their treatments. He was sitting in a chair in an incoherent mental state most of the time.

A minister who visited hospitals asked if he could work with this man. The hospital authorities agreed.

One day the pastor found this man Ricci in a rare coherent moment. The pastor led Ricci to Christ. He responded more and more enthusiastically with each visit, but shortly after his conversion to Christianity, he asked the pastor why the swear words, dirty jokes, dirty pictures and his desire to drink were still there in his mind. The pastor said, "A great offense is the best defense." The pastor asked the man, "Do you know of anyone, who is not a Christian, who Satan would not want removed from his kingdom?" The man had one person in particular in mind and said, "Yes, I do!" The pastor said, "Each time you have wrong thoughts, go on the offense and "target pray" for that individual to become a Christian. It's a great way to defend yourself against Satan's attacks."

Each time Ricci had those debilitating immoral thoughts he would go on the offense and "target pray" specifically for that individual. The pastor saw Ricci a few days later and was thrilled. Ricci asked the pastor what had happened because he was being freed from all that junk that had been in his mind for so long.

The story made sense to Monica. She went home with a mission to pray for the salvation of a non-Christian friend each time Satan would give her immoral thoughts when she was physically involved with her husband. I received a victory letter from her explaining that the Lord was now using her husband to provide physical satisfaction in their relationship. This had never happened before in their entire ten years of marriage. Most of all, Monica appreciated how the Lord Jesus saved her life as she invested in other people through prayer. A great offense is truly a great defense against Satan, the real enemy.

The first hit this inning by Betty came from the authority of His name and the power of His blood, The second hit that Carol had came from not being aware of the many different wicked pitches the enemy throws and having to use the authority of His name and the power of His blood to get the hit. The third hit by Monica came from going on the offense by bringing to the throne of God the name of a person who is not a Christian. Here again, it's important to keep your eye on the ball that Satan throws. Once Satan throws the pitch, that's all he can do.

Hey, those were three great hits that inning. It's good to know who the real enemy is so we can use the authority God has given us. Christ's name is on that bat. There is power in His name. It is sad to see others have such a difficult time with Satan, the enemy. He is a defeated foe. It's wonderful to enter into the victory the Lord has already provided.

Have you had wrong thoughts? Do you want to make the last out of the inning? Go on the offense with God's power and bring into captivity the wrong thought and target pray for one of your non- Christian friends.

28th Inning

She 'Identified' With Jesus This Inning

I have seen and heard many bizarre things, but this situation heads the list. The power of God becomes very evident as you watch the Lord Jesus win the game with His love. Myra looked at her situation from God's point of view and saw it from His eyes. Therefore, He filled her with His Spirit. What did Myra see?

I was speaking in Wisconsin, and Myra, a young married woman, in her late twenties spoke with me. Myra said that her husband, Fred, brought a woman (mistress) home with him. Fred wanted Myra to cook and clean house for him and April, the mistress. Myra was to sleep in the living room while Fred and April were going to sleep in the bedroom.

In my mind I was thinking, "Can this be real? In the first place, what would give Fred the idea that Myra would put up with such infidelity? Fred must have been hoping that Myra would leave.

Myra was an attractive woman, therefore my next thought was, 'Is Fred blind, and what does April look like?' Myra told me that she had hoped this series of messages would have some answers as to what she should do that

209

would glorify God. I showed Myra, I Peter 3:1-4 "Wives, fit in with your husbands' plans; for then if they refuse to listen when you talk to them about the Lord, they will be won by your respectful, pure behavior. Your godly lives will speak to them better than any words. Don't be concerned about the outward beauty that depends on jewelry, or beautiful clothes, or hair arrangement. Be beautiful inside, in your hearts, with the lasting charm of a gentle and quiet spirit that is so precious to God." (TLB)

I asked Myra what Jesus did on the cross for her.

Myra said, "He took my place on the cross and died there for my sins,"

I told Myra that our sins nailed Jesus to the cross, and while we were nailing Him there He looked down at us and said, "I love you." John 15:13 says, " The greatest love is shown when a person lays down his life for his friends:… "(NKJV) Then Jesus did just that.

I said, "If you want to look at it from God's vantage point, imagine in your mind handing Fred and April the hammer and spikes. As they are nailing you to the cross with their sins, do what Jesus did when we nailed Him there with our sins, and say, 'Forgive them for they know not what they do', and then say, 'I love you'."

A few days later God gave Myra the desire to buy April a Bible. Myra told April she loved her and was praying for her. Convicted of wrongdoing, April told Myra, "I can't stay here and continue to do this to you. I never met a woman like you. I truly expected you to leave when your husband brought me home to live with him in your house. I don't understand you, but I respect you. I will not stay and do this to you anymore. April hugged Myra, took the Bible, packed her things and left.

Fred came home, and seeing that April was gone, he blew sky high. Myra could hardly believe how Fred could be so into himself that he wanted both a wife and a mistress.

It was an encouragement to me to see Myra hate the sin, but love the sinner.

Fred could not stand what had happened, so he pursued April. She refused to be involved with Fred. After all, what might Fred do to her in the future? April saw true Christianity in action and had her own Bible to read for the first time in her life. This was the beginning of a new life for April; she had taken a stand for God.

Fred illustrates the depth of degradation in the lower nature of a man. Paul describes the nature in Rom. 7:18-25 "I know I am rotten through and through so far as my old sinful nature is concerned. No matter which way I turn I can't make myself do right. I want to but I can't. When I want to do good, I don't; and when I try not to do wrong, I do it anyway. Now if I am doing what I don't want to, it is plain where the trouble is: sin still has me in its evil grasp. It seems to be a fact of life that when I want to do what is right, I inevitably do what is wrong. I love to do God's will so far as my new nature is concerned; but there is something else deep within me, in my lower nature, that is at war with my mind and wins the fight and makes me a slave to the sin that is still within me. In my mind I want to be God's willing servant, but instead I find myself still enslaved to sin. So you see how it is: my new life tells me to do right, but the old nature that is still inside me loves to sin. Oh, what a terrible predicament I'm in! Who will free me from my slavery to this deadly lower nature? Thank God! It has been done by Jesus Christ our Lord. He has set me free." (TLB)

The Lord does not remove the lower nature, as bad as it is, when one becomes a Christian. The Lord's power over the lower nature is what proves, to this skeptical world, how truly great God is, and how His power is revealed in the spirit-filled Christian. Myra was a wonderful example of the spirit-filled woman as she looked down from her cross.

The Lord says that a non-Christian has a lower nature that showed itself in Fred's life. Only God will be able to get through to Fred. God used Myra and her response to show Fred His power in her life because she trusted Jesus as her Savior and Lord.

I'm sure God will use that picture of what Myra did to show Fred the reality of Christ's death on the cross. When we allow the power of God through the Holy Spirit to control our lower nature, we enjoy the fantastic benefit of the victorious life, a testimony that can draw the non-Christian to Christ as we lift Him up in His rightful place. Have you been on the cross lately? If we want to be like Jesus, we must also go through some of the suffering He went through so we can 'identify' with Him.

29th Inning

This Pitcher Finally
Gained Control

This is the last "Inning", "But The Game Goes On…………."

It is my prayer that anyone with an anger problem will be helped in the last inning of play. In the first inning of this book we saw what a wife did to deal with an angry husband. In this last inning, I will explain what God did to help me with my own personal bout with anger. I had a temper before I was a Christian and thought that God would take my anger and my swearing away. He took the swearing away in a year and a half, but my anger stayed with me. I used to put my fist through walls, throw shoes and act like a spoiled brat.

Satan took advantage of my being a baby Christian. He quoted and twisted scripture to Jesus in the book of John so why wouldn't he twist scripture to cause me to believe a lie. I was thrilled with the story of Paul in II Cor 2 7-11 "a thorn in the flesh was given to me, a messenger of Satan to buffet me, lest I be exalted above measure. Concerning this thing I pleaded with the Lord three times that it might depart from me. And He said to me, "My grace is sufficient for you, for

My strength is made perfect in weakness. Therefore most gladly I will rather boast in my infirmities, that the power of Christ may rest upon me. Therefore I take pleasure in infirmities, in reproaches, in needs, in persecutions, in distresses, for Christ's sake. For when I am weak, then I am strong."

I had believed a lie that the Lord gives everybody a thorn in the flesh to keep them humble. When I would get angry I humbled myself by admitting I was wrong to God and my family. I asked God and my family to forgive me, and I was given God's power to go for another two weeks before I blew it again. I thought God gave me this thorn to keep me humble.

After I asked Jesus to be my Savior and Lord, I noticed that within a year and a half, I was not swearing anymore. I also noticed that my every-other-week anger was not gone. I knew how to ask God to forgive me for I John 1:9 states, "If we confess our sins, He is faithful and just to forgive us *our* sins and to cleanse us from all unrighteousness." (NKJV) Then I would ask my family to forgive me to satisfy Acts 24:16. "And herein do I exercise myself, to have always a conscience void of offence toward God, and *toward* men." (KJV)

What was the truth? I had one of those special conversations with God, which went like this:

"I said, "Lord, I don't get it. You took my swearing away, why haven't you taken my anger?"

He said, "You have believed for years that I gave you the thorn of anger just because I gave Paul a thorn. Jon, did the thorn I gave Paul hurt anyone else?"

I said, "No one knows exactly what the thorn was, but I don't see in scripture where his thorn hurt anyone else."

God said, "The thorn of anger you say I gave you; does it hurt anyone else?"

I said, "Yes, it hurts my wife, my children and anyone else near by."

He said, "Then that's proof it isn't from Me. If a thorn is from Me it affects the principal party, no one else. Jon, you have believed a lie all these years. Ignorance of the law is no excuse.

The Lord went on to say, "Jon, you were a pitcher in baseball; tell Me, how many strikes to get the batter out?"

I said, "Three."

He said, Right! Since you became a Christian you have not thrown the third strike to get "anger" out.

I asked, "What were the first two strikes I threw?"

Jesus asked, "You believed I defeated Satan."

I said, "Yes!"

He said, "Strike one. "Do you believe I'm on the throne of your life?"

I said, "Yes!" He said, "Strike two."

Then He asked, "What, then, is the reason for your propensity to jump over Me and take things into your own hands? Could it be that you are being infl uenced by the iniquity of the forefathers?"

I asked, "Where is that in your Word, and what is iniquity?"

He said, "It's in Jeremiah 14:20 "We acknowledge, O LORD, our wickedness And the iniquity of our fathers, For we have sinned against You." (NKJV) Iniquity is likened as unto rebellion and rebellion is liken to witchcraft."

It is important to remember that by acknowledging the iniquity of our forefathers, we are not forgiving their rebellion, nor are we guilty because of their sin. We are simply agreeing with God about sin and asking Him to remove its consequences from us and from our children."

God lifted the curse that had been past down to the third and fourth generation in Ezekiel 18:20 "The soul who sins shall die. The son shall not bear the guilt of the father."

The Lord continued, "I lifted that curse, but the influence

of your father remains. If you will acknowledge and agree with me about the iniquity of your forefathers influence, as you acknowledge and agree with Me in I John 1:9 when you sin, you will notice a remarkable change."

I asked, "Lord, you always have a hand in glove scripture to back up what you say. Where in the Bible is there something I can see that gives me the picture?"

The Lord said, "Remember in Numbers 21:9 "So Moses made a bronze serpent, and put it on a pole; and so it a serpent had bitten anyone, when he looked at the bronze serpent, he lived."

"Jon, if I can dilute the physical poison of a snake to prevent a person from dying, just because he believed what I said and looked at the snake on the pole, don't you think I can dilute any poison of influence from your forefathers to give you victory over anger?"

I thanked the Lord for the picture of victory. This was the prayer I prayed that stopped the cycle of my angry outbursts. *"Dear Lord Jesus, I acknowledge the iniquity of my forefathers. I believe you, and I ask, by the authority of your Name and the power of Your blood, to remove from me and my children any negative influences, any negative consequences. Thank you for doing that right now."*

I didn't feel any different, and I didn't say anything to Bev about what I had done. Three months went by; there was not one incident where my temper cut loose. Then I asked Bev if she noticed anything different about me. She said she noticed two things. One was that I had become sensitive and the other was that I was not defensive anymore. I asked her why she didn't say anything about me not getting angry. Bev said, "Before, you would say something that would hurt my feelings, because you were insensitive. I would tell you about it, and you would defend yourself, and then blow up. What has happened to you?"

I told Bev what happened. Then Bev realized she held grudges. Our family had learned how to cope with her when she went into one of her grumps, so we didn't think much about her behavior. Bev prayed the same prayer I did, and she hasn't held one grudge since then. For both of us the victory started twenty-six years ago and 'the game goes on" in victory.

Is there any area in your life you need to pray about? Is there some infl uence coming down your family tree that has affected your life in a negative way. If so, would you like to claim this prayer as your very own? *"Dear Lord Jesus, I acknowledge the iniquity of my forefathers. I believe you and I ask, by the authority of your Name and the power of Your blood, to remove from me and my children any negative infl uences, any negative consequences. Thank you for doing that right now. In the name of Jesus I pray. Amen*

It is my prayer that you challenged and enjoyed reading this book. The Lord Jesus Christ inspired me to share with you what He did in these many lives, including mine. Yes, it's all about Jesus. I pray that you will play better "In The Big Inning" knowing that the victory is yours through Jesus-Christ our Savior and Lord.

Thank you for reading, "In The Big Inning". I would appreciate hearing from you about what you thought of these stories. Would you recommend that others read this book? Do you believe a person could become a Christian by reading "In The Big Inning"? Did you ask Jesus into your heart while reading this book?

Again, I would appreciate hearing from you.

Give me a call:

Jon Burnham
309-243-9282
Or e-mail me: jonb2@hotmail.com

May the Lord richly bless you as others watch you play "In The Big Inning"!